Hearing the Silence

Hearing the Silence

Jesus on the Edge and God in the Gap—
Luke 4 in Narrative Perspective

BRUCE W. LONGENECKER

With a Foreword by C. Kavin Rowe

CASCADE *Books* • Eugene, Oregon

HEARING THE SILENCE
Jesus on the Edge and God in the Gap—Luke 4 in Narrative Perspective

Copyright © 2012 Bruce W. Longenecker. All rights reserved. Except for brief quotations in critical publications or reviews, no part of this book may be reproduced in any manner without prior written permission from the publisher. Write: Permissions, Wipf and Stock Publishers, 199 W. 8th Ave., Suite 3, Eugene, OR 97401.

Cascade Books
An Imprint of Wipf and Stock Publishers
199 W. 8th Ave., Suite 3
Eugene, OR 97401

www.wipfandstock.com

ISBN 13: 978-1-61097-229-1

Cataloging-in-Publication data:

Longenecker, Bruce W.

    Hearing the silence : Jesus on the edge and God in the gap—Luke 4 in narrative perspective / Bruce W. Longenecker ; with a Foreword by C. Kavin Rowe.

    xiv + 138 p. ; 23 cm. Including bibliographical references and indexes.

    ISBN 13: 978-1-61097-229-1

    1. Bible. N.T. Luke—Criticism, interpretation, etc. 2. Bible. N.T. Luke—Theology. 3. Bible as literature. I. Title.

BS2595.52 L66 2012

Manufactured in the U.S.A.

*To Art and Coral Rupprecht,
who have been there for the first fifty years,*

*and to Mike Parsons,
a friend for the next fifty.*

Contents

Foreword, by C. Kavin Rowe / ix

Preface / xiii

ONE Imagining Gaps: Holes in the Holy Text / 1

TWO Framing the Issue: The Gap in Nazareth / 14

THREE Navigating Strategies: Novel Imagination to the Rescue / 24

FOUR Discovering Patterns: Luke 4:30 and Divine Causality / 38

FIVE Engaging the Audience: Subtlety as Strategy / 61

SIX Releasing the Captives: Eucatastrophe in Jesus-Novels / 72

SEVEN Constructing Arcs: The Christological Fulfillment of Psalm 91 / 84

Appendix 1: Narrations of Acts 14:19–20 / 113

Appendix 2: What if Luke 22:43–44 is Original to Luke's Gospel? / 117

Appendix 3: Luke's Christological Interpretation of Psalm 91:13 / 120

Bibliography / 125

Index of Ancient Sources / 131

Index of Authors / 137

Foreword

Iris Murdoch's aptly titled and important essay "Against Dryness: A Polemical Sketch" argued for the ability of good literature to renew and sustain our moral imagination in ways that straight philosophical or ethical discourse never could. About this she was doubtless right. Murdoch was not so much interested, however, in the way literary work could shed considerable light on textual conundrums. Bruce Longenecker's book *Hearing the Silence* does just this.

It is true that the modern Jesus-novels Longenecker uses to help him read Luke would not necessarily deserve the name "literature" in the more aesthetically elevated sense. But in their imaginative portrayals of Jesus, they nevertheless creatively comment on (or fill in) a strange silence in the Lukan text that has left the more academically inclined stuttering. Precisely because they speak where the academics have not, these Jesus-novels have the ability to generate thought and to foster interpretative ingenuity where it has been lacking in the scholarly world.

Longenecker's chosen verse is well known to all Lukan specialists and to many Bible readers of all kinds. After Jesus' hometown crowd threatens to throw him off a cliff, the Gospel of Luke says, "But he passed through the middle of them and went on his way" (4:30). No further explanation is given, and nothing more is said. Jesus simply passed through the throng of those who were trying to kill him. What, the curious reader might wonder, should we imagine has happened?

Foreword

Hearing the Silence argues that this is exactly the question that Luke desires his readers to ask. Luke is a storyteller, Longenecker says, and repeatedly tells his story in such a way as to invite his readers into the gaps and silences in the narrative, prompting us to include the missing information as part of our careful reading. Jesus-novelists, argues Longenecker, know this implicitly. They therefore craft elaborate scenes in response to this narrative prompting. In this way, the novelists are excellent readers of Luke, and we can learn from them: they respond eagerly to the directives of the Gospel story, and work creatively to make sense of the gap.

Yet, as Longenecker avers, narrative silences or gaps can't be filled by anything whatsoever. There are better and worse readings, better and worse filler. The better is that which pays attention to the wider Lukan Gospel and seeks to "listen" to the silences in the presence of the chorus of the Gospel as a whole. With respect to this task—i.e., gap-filling as the Lukan narrative would direct—the novelists Longenecker treats turn out to do rather poorly. As a whole, their imaginations are not disciplined by the Lukan text, and they fill in Luke's gap with whatever their own stories seem to need.

Longenecker himself, however, writes as an exegete, and in this role attempts to bring out of the text what he thinks its literary and theological norms require. Longenecker's careful attention to Lukan patterns allows him to identify several interconnections of the Gospel narrative that have, by and large, been unnoticed by scholars and novelists alike.

Whether Longenecker is right about all his particular proposals is ultimately of far less importance than his broader observations about the ingredients of good and sensitive reading. Throughout his book, Longenecker teaches both by way of discussion and example what it means to pay close attention to the flow and logic of Luke's narrative. Though one could learn any number of interesting things from *Hearing the Silence*, perhaps that is the most important lesson of all: becoming good enough readers of

Foreword

Luke to hear what is being said in the silences requires close, prolonged, and repeated readings of the story itself.

C. Kavin Rowe
Duke University, The Divinity School

Preface

INTERPRETING THE story of Jesus has been at the center of Christian history for two thousand years. Since the time when a few Jewish fishermen began telling it in the precincts of the Jerusalem Temple in the year 30 CE, the story of Jesus's life has been told and retold in innumerable ways, for an abundance of purposes.

This book contributes to that enterprise by teasing out interpretive aspects of the Jesus story in one particular instance: that is, the events of Luke 4:30. Curiously, although the plotline of that verse has suffered neglect within scholarship, it has nonetheless been the subject of immensely stimulating imaginative reconstructions in historical fictions about Jesus. The analyses and evaluations that are registered in the following chapters arise from the realm of the academy at times and at other times from the realm of historical fiction—that is, Jesus-narratives in the form of novels and, at times, films. The interweaving of data from these two realms (the academy and historical fiction) provides a fertile hybridity or interplay upon which to construct (what is hoped to be) fruitful and engaging proposals regarding the interpretation of the Lukan story and the theology that the Lukan storyline animates.

Why might a dutiful academic (like me, and perhaps some readers of this book) bother to mix academic scholarship with the spurious and undistinguished world of Jesus-novels? For two reasons. First, because at times watching the imaginative reconstructions of modern storytellers has the effect of putting various interpretive issues into sharp relief. It is not beyond the pale to imagine even the most preeminent of scholars learning a thing or two from those who excel in the craft of imaginatively plotting historical storylines. At times, a storyteller might even open up a situation to allow the trained scholar to exercise her own imagination, even if only as a foil. If I propose this as a possibility for scholars, it is only because it has been the case for me on more than one occasion.

The second reason for dabbling in the world of New Testament fiction is much less ostentatious and much more pedestrian—that is, because at times it is just good fun.

If some of that fun is evident to the reader of this book, there are nonetheless significant issues under consideration. In fact, it is my view that, by investigating the strangely under-narrated "escape" of Jesus in Luke 4:30, we ultimately come face to face with some of the deepest literary structures embedded within the Lukan Gospel and with some of the most fundamental theological convictions of the Lukan worldview. The chapters that follow are dedicated to an exploration of these matters.[1]

---

1. My thanks go to David Beary, Tim Brookins, Brian Gamel, William Henderson, Mikeal Parsons, Kavin Rowe, Mike Whitenton, and Nick Zola for providing important and critical feedback on various versions of this book. William Henderson put the bibliography together and assembled the index of authors, and Mike Whitenton assembled the index of ancient sources; for their efforts I am very grateful. I also thank my wife, Fiona Bond, for her loving support.

ONE

Imagining Gaps

Holes in the Holy Text

FILLING HOLES

THE CANONICAL GOSPELS ARE full of holes. This is wholly to be expected, since those Gospel texts are written in story form. Narratives inescapably contain gaps of one sort or another—narrative spaces that require or at least permit auditors and readers to fill those spaces using their imaginative resources. Like nature, readers of narratives abhor a vacuum.

We should not be surprised when gap-filling ventures are applied to the story of Jesus. After all, throughout the whole of human history, probably no other story has been considered at such length and in such depth as the story of Jesus. It is a story that people have loved, and have loved to imagine their way into, throughout the past twenty centuries. The "presence of absences" or narrative gaps within the canonical Gospels has become the occasion for readers to venture imaginatively into those canonical gaps.

Several narrative "vacuums" in the canonical Gospels have been favored by storytellers as being especially suitable for imaginative elaboration. Throughout the centuries, for instance, one of the most favored vacuums in the story of Jesus has been the so-called "hidden years of Jesus"—the years of childhood, adolescence, and adulthood that preceded his public ministry and remain "hidden" to us. The Gospels of Matthew and Luke recount stories of Jesus' birth (Matt 1:18—2:23; Luke 1:26-56; 2:1-40), and Luke's Gospel describes an incident that took place when Jesus was twelve years old (Luke 2:41-52), but beyond those episodes, the "hidden years" of Jesus' pre-ministerial life remain obscure and inaccessible. This is no obstacle to human imagination, however. Storytellers have repeatedly allowed their imagination to wander virtually unrestrained in exploring the otherwise obscure and inaccessible parts of Jesus' "hidden years."[1] Where historians fear to tread, storytellers frequently rush in, especially in cases where the scope for narrative elaboration is vast and the constraints are minimal.

But even when dealing with the time of Jesus' public ministry, novelists and filmmakers frequently fill other gaps as well. And in that enterprise, three main techniques are most commonly used to fill the gaps within the scriptural narrative or to tease out aspects of the scriptural narrative in some fashion. These include three main techniques:

1. *Augmenting Character Depth:* Storytellers will often bestow additional depth to established characters within the Jesus story, drawing out further dimensions within the conventional plotline. This is most frequently done by teasing out complexity within the personalities of figures near to Jesus. Favorites in this regard are Jesus' mother Mary, Jesus' betrayer Judas, Mary Magdalene from whom Jesus banished seven spirits (and who is frequently depicted as being a harlot), or Jesus' disciple Peter. Adding complexity to their characters or complications to their relations with Jesus can provide new narrative intrigue to the traditional story.

---

1. Two well-known examples come from the *Infancy Gospel of Thomas*, in which Jesus forms pigeons out of clay and then sets them off to fly away (2.1-5), followed by the killing of other boys when Jesus gets angry at them and divine power shoots out of him (3.1—4.1).

Imagining Gaps

2. *Augmenting Situational Depth:* Storytellers will often bestow additional depth to a storyline, enhancing the situational dynamics operating within a given scriptural episode. This is frequently done by placing an event within a context that enlarges upon the scriptural text, or through the back-narrating of prior relevant events. In this way, the scriptural episode resonates with new forms of meaning.

3. *Adding New Characters:* Storytellers will often introduce new characters to the scriptural storyline, allowing those invented personalities to enhance the plotline in some fashion or to carry it into new narrative terrain.

Interestingly, each of these three main techniques for narrative enhancement has a foothold in narrative developments within the scriptural Gospels themselves. This is often easy to spot. As scholars almost unanimously agree, the Gospel of Mark was the first canonical Gospel to be written, being used by Matthew and Luke when composing their later Gospels, which incorporated narrative adjustments into the recounting of the life of Jesus.[2] Many of those narrative adjustments fall into at least one the three techniques cited above. A few examples will demonstrate the point (all of which are drawn solely from Luke's Gospel, since the main interest of this book pertains to that Gospel):

Adding relational complexity to figures already established within the Jesus story is evident in a passage like Luke 23:39–43. There, the two men who were crucified with Jesus become differentiated and given distinctive characterizations. Whereas in Mark's Gospel the two are undifferentiated, Luke's Gospel individualizes them. While the first "criminal" taunts and derides Jesus ("Are you not the Messiah? Save yourself and us!"), the other chastises the first for his derision, proclaims Jesus' innocence, and pleads for Jesus to "remember me when you come into your kingdom." With words unknown from other Gospels, Jesus re-

---

2. See especially Goodacre, "Setting in Place the Cornerstone," 19–45.

plies, "Truly I tell you, today you will be with me in Paradise."[3] In this fashion, the plotline of the Markan Gospel is elaborated further in Luke's Gospel by introducing heightened relational dynamics within the narrative.

Adding situational depth by placing an event within a larger narrative context and providing some explanatory back-narration is precisely what we find in a passage like Luke 4:38—5:11. In the Markan Gospel, Jesus calls disciples to him immediately after having been tempted in the wilderness, most famously in his words to Peter, "Follow me and I will make you fish for people" (Mark 1:17). In Mark's version, Jesus calls four fishermen to follow him and the reader is told, "immediately they left their nets and followed him" (1:18; compare 1:20). But why would they be willing to do such a thing? Is there a back-story to this episode that helps explain the disciples' unusual willingness more fully?[4]

Luke addresses the reader's query directly, by adding situational depth. In his retelling of the story, the calling of the fishermen to be Jesus' disciples is preceded by two very important moments that reveal something about Jesus' incredible power. So, Jesus' statement to Peter "from now on you will be catching people" (Luke 5:10) is *preceded by* Jesus healing Peter's mother-in-law (Luke 4:38-40)—an episode that, in the Markan plotline, *follows after* Jesus called Peter to follow him (Mark 1:29-31). In

---

3. Other examples of heightened characterization from Luke might include Luke 20:20–26, where the antagonistic motivation of "the scribes and chief priests" is augmented; or Luke 22:3, where it is simply stated that "Satan entered into Judas"; see also Luke 22:31 ("Simon, Simon, listen! Satan has demanded to sift all of you like wheat").

4. Novelists sometimes think not. So, for instance, LaHaye and Jenkins (*Mark's Story*, 122) narrate the calling of the first disciples in the following fashion, with Peter explaining the situation when Jesus called him, Andrew, James and John to fish for people: "we looked at each other and we simply knew... that we had no choice... God must have put it in our hearts. None of us were out of sorts or unhappy with our lives or looking for anything new or different. This man simply appeared and told us, didn't ask us, to follow Him, and that the time was right. He carried Himself with such authority—and yet with humility—that we somehow understood that we were to go with Him and that our lives would never be the same."

Imagining Gaps

addition to this inversion of sequence, Luke adds other episodes to his plotline to help explain why fishermen would so easily have dropped their livelihood and followed Jesus. Not only does Luke insert the mention of Jesus' many healings and exorcisms in 4:40–41 prior to the calling of his disciples in 5:10, he also elaborates the calling episode itself, infusing it with a back-story throughout 5:1–11. In that episode, the fishermen are shown to have tried valiantly to catch fish, but to no avail; upon Jesus' command to drop their nets back into the waters, their fishing nets are filled to overflowing, to the extent that the boats are even in danger of sinking. Consequently, Peter's subsequent actions are themselves dripping with heavy theological import; we are told that "he fell at Jesus' knees and said, 'Go away from me, Lord; I am a sinful man!'" If the Markan plotline leaves the reader wondering why a fisherman would leave his livelihood to follow Jesus who seems simply to appears on the scene, the Lukan plotline addresses that perplexity by filling narrative gaps, leaving a more satisfying understanding of the cause-and-effect relationships within Jesus' calling of the fishermen.

Adding new characters to the traditional storyline in order to allow those characters to take the plot along different paths is much like what we find in a passage like Luke 23:48. In that single verse, Luke adds mention of a "multitude" of people who, after viewing the crucifixion of Jesus, return home "beating their breasts," thereby implicitly confirming Pilate's view that Jesus was "innocent." This unspecified group of people has been added to the narrative to enhance an important feature of the storyline—the innocence of Jesus is clearly recognizable to those who see things plainly.[5]

---

5. Although not from Luke's Gospel, an indicative example of adding new characters to the plot comes from Matt 20:20–21. In this episode, the sons of Zebedee (James and John) are put forward as being worthy to sit at the right and left hand of Jesus when he enters into his glory. In the Markan narrative, this hare-brained request comes from James and John themselves (Mark 10:25–27). In reworking the Markan narrative, however, Matthew has the request being made by *the mother of* James and John. The Matthean narrative

At times these three techniques will overlap and reinforce each other, of course. This happens in Luke 23:6–16, where Jesus is brought to stand trial before Herod Antipas. Although Herod Antipas has already made an appearance in Luke's Gospel, he appears within the narrative of Jesus' trial in a fashion unparalleled in any other Gospel. This episode of Jesus standing before Herod Antipas adds intrigue to Luke's Gospel in several ways. First, it enhances dramatic irony by having Jesus, who is later crucified as the "king of the Jews" (Luke 23:3, 37–38), stand before the very one who spent much of his career seeking (although ultimately in vain) to earn from Rome the title "king"—a title Rome had bestowed on his father (cf. Luke 1:5). Second, the dramatic irony is enhanced further by the fact that Herod Antipas had already murdered John the Baptist (cf. Luke 3:18–20; 9:7–9) and is said to have been trying to murder Jesus (Luke 13:31), with Jesus calling him a cunning "fox" (Luke 13:32). Notably, although Herod treats Jesus with contempt (putting an elegant robe on him and mocking him), he does not act on his murderous desire to have Jesus removed from the scene but, intriguingly, decides to send Jesus back to Pilate, allowing Pilate to decide Jesus' fate. In this way, Herod has made a gesture that signals his respect for Pilate's authority, and as a consequence "that same day Herod and Pilate became friends with each other; before this they had been enemies" (Luke 23:12). The political drama is high, and in the process Jesus is shown to have been right in his depiction of Herod Antipas as a cunning fox.

Examples of this kind could be multiplied repeatedly, but they are not of ultimate concern here. The point is simply that what we often see happening in later imaginative renderings of the Jesus-story is not unrelated to techniques evidenced by the canonical evangelists themselves—those who were among the

---

is rather charming (after all, what mother doesn't want the best for her sons?), but the intention behind it is most likely to preserve the reputation of two of Jesus' chief disciples by attributing the absent-minded request to someone other than them.

Imagining Gaps

first to retell the established storyline, and who often retold it with fresh narrative creativity. The way the canonical evangelists handled the Jesus-story bears some relationship to what faithful Christians have often done when enhancing that story's narrative plot in modern Jesus-narratives. Canonical evangelists and modern Jesus-narrators often share similar kinds of techniques, and often share similar motivations, having to do with the literary and theological enhancement of the traditional storyline.[6]

But there are also modern Jesus-novelists who retell the Jesus-story for different purposes altogether. Sharing some of the same techniques as those outlined above, these Jesus-narrators do not share the same faith-inspiring motivations as the canonical evangelists. Instead, they use the techniques outlined above to expand upon the Jesus-story in ways that run contrary to the faith-inspiring intention of those evangelists. While most Jesus-narrators have been orthodox Christians seeking to explore and bolster the Christian faith by way of historical fiction, those with little or no Christian commitment are increasingly drawn to the enterprise of retelling the Jesus-story. These include Jesus-narrators from faiths other than Christianity (e.g., Judaism, Islam),[7] whose novels respectfully entertain theological options other than those promoted by traditional forms of Christianity; and they include Jesus-narrators who are plainly antagonistic to

---

6. The point was made by the great British playwright and poet Dorothy L. Sayers (1893-1957), when explaining her method of casting the story of Jesus into a series of 1942 radio plays. As she notes in the introduction to the script (*The Man Born to be King*, 23): "All this involved the taking of some liberties with the Gospel text—the omission of some incidents, the insertion and expansion of others, the provision of background, and what are technically called 'bridges' to link the episodes, and occasional transpositions. For most of these activities there was ample precedent in the Gospels themselves: Matthew and Luke are the great 'transposers'; John, the provider of glosses, backgrounds, and bridges."

7. Jewish Jesus-novelists include: Asch, *The Nazarene*; Mossinsohn, *Judas*; Kassoff, *The Book of Witnesses*; Heym, *Ahasver* (in German); and Gompertz, *A Jewish Novel about Jesus*. The sole Muslim Jesus-novelist known to me is Hussein, *City of Wrong*.

Christianity.[8] As a consequence, "revisionist" Jesus-novels have recently grown in popularity, depicting Jesuses that are not constrained by canonical depictions of him.

This growing interest in the story of Jesus and his followers from non-orthodox novelists is, arguably, due to the attraction of promulgating non-orthodox perceptions of Jesus and Christianity within the genre traditionally thought to be the reserve of Christian orthodoxy. But the enterprise itself is not a new one. These non-orthodox Jesus-novels have their own ancient predecessors in many of the apocryphal Gospels whose intention seems not one of supplementing the canonical Gospels but, in a sense, of supplanting them—Gospels such as the *Gospel of Thomas* or the recently recovered *Gospel of Judas*, both of which are best dated to the second-century CE and both of which betray some influence of "gnostic" sensitivities.[9]

But regardless of the theological "camp" of the various Jesus-narrators, what we see in virtually all of their literary efforts (whether ancient or modern) are attempts to influence the established storyline in order to "freshen it up" in one way or another, for one purpose or another. As a result, the imaginative reconstruction of the Jesus-story has been a thriving industry. In the twentieth century, novels about Jesus and his followers emerged at an average rate of four per year.[10] And the productivity of the Jesus-novel in the early twenty-first century suggests that the

---

8. The most obvious example of this is Saramago, *The Gospel according to Jesus Christ*. Others of note in this category include: Graves, *King Jesus*; Harrison, *The Memoirs of Jesus Christ*; Fortney, *The Thomas Jesus*; Ricci, *Testament*; Freke and Gandy, *The Gospel of the Second Coming*. On Saramago's novel, see Longenecker, "The Challenge of a Hopeless God."

9. In "gnostic" frames of reference, the created order is despised to the extent that salvation requires initiatives to by-pass the created order altogether. As a consequence, the humanity of Jesus is generally compromised in gnostic worldviews. On the *Gospel of Thomas*, see especially Perrin, *Thomas*; on the *Gospel of Judas*, see Gathercole, *The Gospel of Judas*; Wright, *Judas and the Gospel of Jesus*.

10. I owe this data to my former PhD student, Meg Ramey, in dialogue with Zeba Crook, both of whom have done research into Jesus-novels.

Imagining Gaps

pouring of imaginative expertise into the gaps of the Gospels will continue to be a creative enterprise well into the future, perhaps as much as it has been in the past.

WHAT WE'LL BE DOING

Imaginative reconstruction of the Jesus-story lies at the heart of this book. In what follows, one passage from Luke will be the primary focus of attention in one way or another. The interpretation of Luke 4:28–30, and in particular the curiosity that resides in the climax of those verses in 4:30, forms the spine that runs throughout the various chapters of this book. The sequence of the argument will unfold in the following fashion:

1. Chapter 2 will explore dimensions of the narrative in Luke 4:28–30, noting in particular the presence of a gap in the narration of the events recounted there.

2. Chapter 3 will outline a series of attempts to amplify the plotline of that single verse, demonstrating four strategies Jesus-novelists often employ when filling the gap with content.

3. Chapters 4 and 5 will propose another way to fill the gap of Luke 4:30, one that falls into alignment with the theological character of the Lukan narrative.

4. Chapter 6 will outline the plotlines of the few Jesus-novels that narrate the event of Luke 4:30 in ways proposed in chapters 4 and 5.

5. Chapter 7 will push the proposal further, adding to the mixture yet another narrative dimension of the events recounted in Luke 4:30 in relation to another episode in the Lukan Gospel.

Before moving to those chapters, however, a few words of explanation are appropriate here. First, throughout this book, I refer to the canonical evangelists by the names traditionally ascribed to them (i.e., Matthew, Mark, Luke, John), regardless of the merits of that nomenclature.

Second, the following terms regularly appear: "reader," "audience," "auditor," "hearer." Usually these terms are used relatively interchangeably. The term that causes me some uneasiness, however, is "reader." In the ancient world, there were very few "readers"; in the oral/aural culture of the first century CE, a text was read to an audience of hearers or auditors. Nonetheless, I retain the use of the term "reader" since it facilitates an easier presentation of the argument at certain points.

Third, one issue is addressed at various points through the following chapters, but deserves some initial airing at this point. The proposal of this book errs on the side of thinking that something can be said about what certain features of the Gospel of Luke "mean" and "do" in their position within the unfolding of that Gospel. This matter of "meaning," of course, has been the subject of intense debate for the past half-century or so, regarding the extent to which a text can be studied in relation to the interests of its author. Extreme skeptics assert that interpretations are inevitably influenced by the interpreter's own social location and vested interests, and ultimately by certain power structures to which the interpreter is inevitably indebted. When an interpreter operates under the guise that a text itself "has meaning," she is blinded to the fact that her interpretation is little more than a means of reinforcing power structures that have implicitly informed her reading.[11]

This is a very important nexus to be aware of, to be sure, and represents a clarion call to all interpreters that, as Rudolf Bultmann long ago asserted (as did many before him), there is no such thing as "presuppositionless exegesis."[12] Even if at times we find it tantalizing to speak of the almost "inexhaustible

---

11. See, for instance, *The Postmodern Bible* by "The Bible and Culture Collective."

12. See his essay "Is Exegesis without Presuppositions Possible?"

Imagining Gaps

hermeneutical potential" of a text,[13] the inevitable result of this should not be to denude completely the text and/or the author of all influence in the hermeneutical process. The long-established recognition that subjectivity is inevitable within interpretation should, of course, compel us to be cautious in our expectations about what interpreters offer, and to be probing in our assessment of how interpretations may derive from and be aligned with certain structures of power. But knee-jerk reactions calling for the death of the text and/or the author (calls that themselves are highly politicized and hardly unaligned to certain power structures) are not a methodological improvement.[14]

Instead of getting enmeshed at the extremes of this issue, the best path is traversed somewhere between the two—that is, between staunch skepticism that foregrounds interpretive subjectivity, on the one hand, and, on the other hand, a gullible optimism based on an illusory quest for historical objectivity.[15] Robert Alter rightly gives voice to a reasonable viewpoint that coincides largely with my own:

> there must be some grounds for discriminating between plausible interpretations and preposterous ones. We are able to make such a distinction above all because a work of literature is a highly articulated verbal construct, not a Rorschach blot onto which everyone can project his own fantasies . . . [M]any of those who like to think of themselves as the vanguard of contemporary criticisms appear unwilling to conceive a middle ground between the insistence on one authoritative reading and the allowing of all readings.[16]

---

13. Hays, *The Moral Vision of the New Testament*, 1.

14. On the death of the author, see especially Barthes, "The Death of the Author"; relatedly, Ricoeur, "Language as Discourse."

15. A related issue, but one that cannot be explored here, is the role of Scripture within communities of faith, where a quest for authorial meaning has validity alongside a variety of other forms of textual meaning.

16. Alter, *The Pleasures of Reading in an Ideological Age*, 220–21.

While we should not lull ourselves into imagining that our interpretations can escape the inevitable grasp of subjectivity, neither should we allow that grasp of subjectivity to strip the interpretive discipline of discourse concerning the nature of textual controls.[17] This "middle way" is the route proposed by advocates of "practical realism," for instance, in its opposition to naïve historical positivism, on the one hand, and, on the other, naïve postmodern relativism.[18]

Perhaps, then, the discipline of biblical studies is at the point where more voices will echo the sentiments of someone like Philip Esler, who has recently argued that "authorial intention [must be retained] as an essential feature in New Testament interpretation."[19] He elaborates in this way:

> While a text will certainly have different meanings in contexts beyond those of its first audience, this does not mean that it escapes the horizon of its author. Historical analysis will always reveal, though imperfectly, that horizon sufficiently enough for the text to convey meaning. Even in the case of communication by the actual living voice between two speakers in one another's presence, communication is never perfect and there is always some slippage of meaning. Each speaker will not say quite what he or she intended and his or her message will, to some extent, be misunderstood. That is simply one aspect of being human; it is no reason to rule out of court the pos-

---

17. Oddly, even those who have no confidence in a text's stability seem nonetheless to expect their readers to comprehend the meaning that their articles and books are meant to convey. No one, not even the most hardened skeptic of textual stability, would imagine that the contract she signed with her employers should be subject to whims of relativist interpretation; quite simply, that text (i.e., the contract) has certain parameters within which it is to be interpreted. Failure to operate within those parameters is recognized as a transgression by the courts of law.

18. See Appleby *et al.*, *Telling the Truth about History*.

19. Esler, *New Testament Theology*, 117. See his extended defense of this charge in "The Place of New Testament Authors in Interpretation" (88–118) and "The Author and Authorial Intention in the New Testament" (182–87).

Imagining Gaps

sibility of understanding a textual communication from the past.[20]

Francis Watson argues along similar lines. Noting that there "are always a variety of ways in which the semantic potential of a scriptural text may be realized," Watson nonetheless insists that a text's semantic potential is not unendingly elastic; in fact, "it is wrong to imagine that the text itself is no more than a blank screen onto which readers project their various concerns . . . To interpret is always to interpret with a text, and it is also to be *constrained* by the text."[21]

The arguments that form the core of this book are, then, to be judged on the basis of the extent to which they are seen to be constrained by the Lukan text. The reader will judge whether subjectivity or textual constraint predominates in the proposals that follow, which are offered to the public arena for consideration and, of course, for disagreement, should textual constraints be seen to override them.[22]

---

20. Esler, *New Testament Theology*, 185.

21. Watson, *Paul and the Hermeneutics of Faith*, 4, emphasis original. So too Moessner has demonstrated that ancient authors sought to "manage" how their literary works were being comprehended; see his "Managing the Audience," esp. 180–81.

22. In view of the subjectivity involved in reading meaning from a text, the arena of public discourse needs to be as vibrantly robust and as broadly represented as possible, providing "checks and balances" on proposed readings in consonance with the text's own constraints. A healthy disagreement about whether and what a text "means" and how it is put into the service of larger conglomerations of power is inevitable in the arena of the humanities. Interpreters do not need to be infantilized by the prospect of subjectivity so much as to be educated about it, to engage in self-reflection about their interpretive output, and to wear tough skin as they launch interpretive proposals about what the text might mean into the rightly-diverse and rightly-critical public arena.

TWO

Framing the Issue
The Gap in Nazareth

THE SINGLE VERSE OF Luke 4:30 has not received full attention in scholarly discussion. Perhaps that neglect arises in part from the fact that the verse is full of narrative ambiguity and, in fact, narrative oddity. But it is precisely because of this narrative ambiguity and oddness that the verse has some attraction in a sphere rather tangential to the realm of academic scholarship—that is, in imaginative reconstructions of the life of Jesus in film and fiction. This chapter canvasses the narrative flow of Luke 4:28–30, laying foundations for the chapters that follow.

THE NARRATION OF LUKE 4:28–30

The Lukan account of Jesus in the Nazareth synagogue (Luke 4:16–30) expands on the version found in the earlier Gospel of Mark. In Mark 6:1–6, the episode is brief, undeveloped, and results only in antagonism between Jesus and his townspeople. In Mark's Gospel, the episode ends in this way (Mark 6:3–6):

> They took offense at him. Then Jesus said to them, "Prophets are not without honor, except in their hometown, and among their own kin, and in their own house." And he could do no deed of power there, except that he

Framing the Issue

laid his hands on a few sick people and cured them. And he was amazed at their unbelief.[1]

What the Gospel of Mark recounts in six verses is significantly expanded upon in the Gospel of Luke, which recounts the episode in fifteen verses. In the process, the situational complexity is noticeably enhanced in the Lukan account. That later account displays heightened expansions, both in the way it depicts relationships between the episode's characters (through extended dialogue between Jesus and the people of Nazareth) and by its intensification of the episode's dramatic action (through an extended plotline). In the Lukan version of the Nazareth incident, Jesus (1) reads publicly from Isaiah 61 about the Spirit of the Lord empowering his own ministry, (2) proclaims that the passage is fulfilled that day, and (3) engages in a protracted dispute with others in the synagogue, including extended discussion of Elijah and Elisha. Moreover, if the main body of the Lukan episode is markedly more developed than its Markan predecessor, the same is true for the Lukan conclusion of the episode. The tension is heightened in Luke 4:28-29, which has no counterpart in the Gospel of Mark: "Hearing these things, all in the synagogue were filled with rage. Rising up, they threw him out of the city, and led him to the brow of the hill on which their city was built, so that they might hurl him off the cliff." Then the episode's climax appears in Luke 4:30, again without a Markan precedent: "But he passed through the midst of them and went on his way."

In narrative terms, this account is, at first blush, completely unsatisfactory, since the climax in Luke 4:30 does not follow on neatly from its narrative context. The build-up to the climax is depicted cleanly and clearly in Luke 4:28-29, and is full of narrative tension, owing to the forceful and violent handling that the people of Nazareth inflict on Jesus. They are enraged, they rise up against him, they throw him out of the city, they drag him to the very edge of a cliff, and they are wholly intent on throwing

---

1. The translation used here and throughout is the NRSV.

him down from the cliff, whereupon they would pelt him with stones until there was no life left in him. If this narrative tension is rarely done justice to by academic scholars, it is nonetheless easily grasped by Jesus-novelists, who excel in the craft of imaginative plotting of narrative storylines.

Some of the more elaborate reconstructions will be entertained in chapters that follow (chapters 3 and 6 below), but for now, a few of the more simple reconstructions of Luke 4:28–29 can be registered here in order to demonstrate the way that the build-up of conflict in the Lukan narrative is amplified by Jesus-novelists, even when the amplification is minimalistic (relatively speaking). Resorting to depictions of the scene in Jesus-novels helps us to visualize the tension of the Lukan scene through imaginative amplification. So, one Jesus-novelist recounts the episode in this way: "[T]hey were half pushing, half carrying their former carpenter out of the synagogue and down the road to where the hillside has fallen away and there is a sheer drop into the valley below," adding that "[t]here they held Jesus, just inches from certain death."[2]

Another Jesus-novelist depicts it similarly: "The crowd was pushing toward a place where the ground dropped away, and Jesus stumbled ahead of them, resisting and giving way and calling members of the crowd by name . . . They had Jesus on the very edge of the precipice, the ground giving and crumbling beneath his feet."[3] The drama is acute and intense. A single individual is in the clutches of an enraged mob, a throng united in its singular intent to throw him from the edge of the cliff

---

2. Harrison, *Oriel's Diary*, 50.

3. Monhollon, *Divine Invasion*, 60. Neither of Anne Rice's two Jesus-novels includes this incident, but her second may well be preparing the groundwork for a depiction of the incident in a forthcoming Jesus-novel. In her second Jesus novel *The Road to Cana*, Rice repeatedly depicts the people of Nazareth as quick to draw the blood of anyone whom they dislike, for even the most outlandish reasons. Nazareth is a place "where they stone children on the say-so of other children" (89).

Framing the Issue

whereupon, if he didn't die from the fall, he would be stoned to death by the mob above.

As the situation is depicted in Luke 4:29, the auditor of the Lukan narrative is evidently to imagine Jesus as virtually standing on tip-toe as his oppressors dangle him next to the craggy precipice.[4] Narratively speaking, everything is as it should be: clean, clear, pronounced, exhilarating, and therefore captivating. But all this changes in Luke 4:30. The conflict that has animated the acute drama of Luke 4:28–29 simply dissipates in Luke 4:30, in what looks like a distinctly inferior conclusion to the intensity of the conflict depicted in the two preceding verses. As one academic writes, "In some mysterious manner, left unexplained by Luke, at the point of what appeared to be certain death, Jesus simply walks away through the crowd unhindered and unharmed."[5]

This "mysterious" and "unexplained" feature might, at first glance, appear to be a conspicuously mediocre moment in Luke's narration, one absent of believable cause-and-effect plot chains. But is this, in fact, the case? Is the narration here sub-standard? Or is there more to things than first meets the eye? That's the question that will be explored in what follows.

---

4. That Jesus is in the clutches of an angered mob and at the very point of death is reinforced by the parallel between this incident and the same author's account of the killing of Stephen in Acts 7. Luke uses the same expression in each passage to speak of his protagonists being thrown out of the city: "throwing him outside the city" (ἐκβαλόντες ἔξω τῆς πόλεως) in Acts 7:58 and "they threw him outside the city" (ἐξέβαλον αὐτὸν ἔξω τῆς πόλεως) in Luke 4:29—the only two places where the verb "to throw out" (ἐκβάλλειν) and the noun "city" (πόλις) appear together in the whole of the New Testament. The story of Stephen illustrates how brutal Luke imagines the process of throwing someone out of a city to be, and how perilous he imagines the expected fate of those who are thrown out of cities. Compare also the account in Acts 14, discussed in Appendix 1 below, in which Paul is stoned and then dragged out of the city (ἔσυρον ἔξω τῆς πόλεως).

5. Cunningham, *Through Many Tribulations*, 65.

Hearing the Silence

NARRATIVE CONNECTIVITY AND ITS ABSENCE

It is clear that Luke 4:30 is "under-narrated." It is also the case that leaving such a prominent and curious gap in the plotline is not typical of Luke's normal narrative style. At many points (although certainly not all points), Luke tends to close up gaps in his narrative. This is evident, for instance, in the account of Jesus calling disciples to follow him (Luke 5:1–11). As noted in chapter 1 above, in his retelling of that account, Luke seems intent on avoiding a situation in which his audience is left to wonder about relatively obvious gaps in the Jesus-story. Why did the disciples immediately leave their nets and follow Jesus? We might postulate all kinds of reasons. But Luke closes down the opportunity to speculate by providing a compelling back-narrative that forecloses all other options. In the Nazareth incident, however, just the opposite is evident.

Of course, it might be that Luke has simply left a gaping hole in the narrative of Luke 4:30 without noticing it. While this option needs always to be considered, it is usual for narrative critics to adopt this option only after all other options have been explored and rendered unworkable. In his book *The Birth of the Lukan Narrative*, Mark Coleridge makes the point this way:

> One of the underlying assumptions [of narrative analysts when encountering gaps in the storyline] is that the evangelist is in control of his material, that . . . he is more master than slave of the elements of his text. This would mean, for instance, that where fissures, gaps or elisions appear in the text, the initial assumption would be that the author wants them to be there, and the critical question is therefore "why?" There will of course be times when the critic can no longer maintain an assumption of this kind. At that point, there is no choice but to abandon the initial assumption . . . But it is a question of what initial assumption the critic brings to the task; and narratival criticism begins with the assumption that the

Framing the Issue

evangelist has over his material a control which if not absolute is nonetheless real.[6]

It is, of course, the case that Luke leaves gaps in his narrative, and some of these would have been unnoticed by him, or unimportant to him, or unintentional on his part.[7] But it is also the case that on occasion those gaps seem highly intentional—the case of the ending of the Acts of the Apostles, for instance, will be considered in chapter 5 below (with Acts being the second of the two Lukan contributions to the New Testament).[8] Moreover, notice needs to be given to Luke's handling of material earlier in his Gospel, where he demonstrates keen interest in making explicit connections within plotlines. So, for instance, as one scholar has noted:

> Instead of having characters suddenly appear somewhere or being directed to go elsewhere, as in Matthew, Luke moves his characters from place to place with narrative logic. Zachariah has reason for being in the temple and for coming out of it, Mary's trip to Elizabeth is described, there is movement among Zachariah's neighbors and kinfolk, Joseph has a specific reason for going to Bethlehem, the shepherds discuss their decision to visit the manger after the angel's announcement to them. Events in Luke are connected, in other words—history, or the reporting of history, or the creation of literature, involves not only recording events or their causes, but also describing what happens to people in time and space as events unravel.[9]

Not only is the narrative gap of Luke 4:30 remarkably "noticeable," then, it is also notably different from the high degree of "connectivity" that is displayed already within Luke's Gospel.

---

6. Coleridge, *The Birth of the Lukan Narrative*, 17.

7. It might be, for instance, that the reference to what Jesus did in Capernaum in Luke 4:23 is a case in point, since there is no episode in the preceding narrative that took place in that town.

8. For a study of Lukan narrative gaps, see Maxwell, *Hearing between the Lines*.

9. Gros Louis, "The Jesus Birth Stories," 280.

Perhaps, then, the curious lack of connectivity at the conclusion of the Nazareth incident taunts the audience into asking, "How did that happen?" Inspiring curiosity is one of the functions of narrative gaps. According to literary theorist Wolfgang Iser, when a reader experiences a gap in a narrative's plotline, "the imagination is automatically mobilized, thus increasing the constitutive activity of the reader, who cannot help but try and supply the missing links."[10] In his book *The Poetics of Biblical Narrative*, Meir Sternberg says much the same. According to him, a literary work "consists of bits and fragments to be linked and pieced together in the process of reading: it establishes a system of gaps that must be filled in. This gap-reading [can involve] intricate linkages of elements, which the reader performs automatically, [or can involve] intricate networks that are figured out consciously, laboriously, hesitantly, and with constant modifications in the light of additional information disclosed in later stages of the reading."[11]

This function of narrative gaps is not just a phenomenon of modern literature, but has strong foundations within the archives of ancient literature. In fact, as Kathy Reiko Maxwell has recently noted, "Audience-oriented criticism, while named only recently, is an ancient phenomenon as old as story telling itself ... [A]ncient speakers and writers left holes or gaps in their narratives, encouraging the audience to become 'fellow-workers' ... with the speaker."[12] She continues: "[A]t times authors use silence to speak to their audience. A gap, an unexpected hole in the presentation, impels the audience to do more than merely receive

---

10. Iser, *The Act of Reading*, 186.

11. Sternberg, *The Poetics of Biblical Narrative*, 186. He continues on page 187: "In works of greater complexity, the filling-in of gaps becomes much more difficult and therefore more conscious and anything but automatic."

12. Maxwell, *Hearing between the Lines*, xiii, where she cites Plutarch *Mor.* 48.14; see her fuller discussion of the antiquity of this technique on pages 27–117. See also Marguerat, *The First Christian Historian*, 206–16. For a modern discussion of the same phenomenon, see especially Iser, *The Act of Reading*, 180–231.

the story. If not provided in the narrative, the missing information must come from elsewhere. The silence of intentional gaps invites the audience to speak, to engage the unfolding rhetoric, and to become part of the story themselves."[13]

If in 4:30 Luke is employing an ancient technique of using a silence to speak to his audience, what is he trying to say? What function does that silent gap perform? How is the audience's imagination expected to come into play, as the audience itself gets drawn into the process of providing the missing link within the narrative?

JESUS-NARRATIVES NEGOTIATE THE MISSING LINK: A FIRST LOOK

If the Lukan ending to the Nazareth incident is "under-narrated," this is not what we find in the ending of Mark's account of the incident, as quoted above—an ending that is replicated almost exactly in the later Gospel of Matthew (13:53–58). In the Gospel of Mark, although the people of Nazareth take offence at Jesus, the episode concludes with Jesus simply marveling at their lack of faith. There is no dramatic lynching and no unexplained unraveling of the mob's appalling intentions. If Mark's recounting of the incident is not as gripping as Luke's, the Gospel of Mark nonetheless offers a fitting and appropriate account of the incident, free from gaping holes in the action and devoid of unsatisfying plotline descriptions.

It is notable, then, that when Jesus-novelists attempt to fictionalize the Nazareth incident, they generally gravitate toward the more elaborate and tantalizing Lukan incident, rather than toward its more basic Markan precursor.[14] The narrative drama

13. Maxwell, *Hearing between the Lines*, 1.
14. I know of no modern novelist who fictionalizes the Markan version of the Nazareth incident. To my knowledge, only two narratives mention the Markan version in undeveloped fashion, but each also depicts the Lukan version in a separate chapter, as if these were two separate events. See Gompertz, *A Jewish Novel about Jesus*, 70, 78; and Mailer, *The Gospel according to the Son*, 64 (where Luke 4 is greatly rewritten) and ibid., 100–101.

of the Lukan version offers scope for the imagination almost to run wild. Little wonder, then, that instead of replicating the Markan episode of Jesus in the Nazareth synagogue, Jesus-novelists usually find the Lukan episode to be more congenial to their narrative interests. Not only does it have enhanced conflict and dramatic action, but it also has a notably peculiar ending that draws dramatic attention to itself.

Precisely this peculiarity of ending, however, makes for difficulties when narrating the incident. This is evident, for instance, in the way Luke's Nazareth incident is handled in the Jesus-films that seek to re-enact it on the silver screen. For instance, in Martin Scorsese's 1988 adaptation of Nikos Kazantzakis's *The Last Temptation of Christ*, Jesus engages in an extended dispute with the people of Nazareth (1.14:56 through 1.17:21, in dialogue that shows almost no indebtedness to the biblical witness), but at no point is he dragged to the edge of a cliff; instead, after a stone is thrown at him, he and his disciples take the hint and depart from Nazareth.

Much the same is the depiction of the event in George Stevens's 1965 film *The Greatest Story Ever Told* (1.36:51 through 1.40:52). One stone is thrown at Jesus, hitting his back as he walks away from his townspeople; he turns and looks at them one final time, then carries on his way out of Nazareth. There's no dramatic grasping of him by the people of Nazareth, no dragging him off, and no cliff. Evidently, in order to avoid having to explain how Jesus could have released himself from the clutches of his neighbors and gone on his way through their midst, Stevens chose simply to lessen the dramatic conflict of the biblical narrative.

The difficulty that directors of Jesus-films have in narrating the Lukan Nazareth episode is subtly testified to by the 1979 film *Jesus* (also known as *The Jesus Film*), directed by Peter Sykes, John Heyman, and John Krisch. This film maintains the drama of the Lukan narrative, depicting the people of Nazareth as grabbing Jesus in the synagogue and dragging him off to a nearby cliff. And the cinematic episode ends with Jesus walking on his

Framing the Issue

way, leaving the people of Nazareth behind. All this matches the depiction of things in Luke 4:28–30. But how does Jesus release himself from the grasp of an enraged mob? The film gives no answer. In fact, at the key moment when the escape happens, the film cuts away from the events transpiring on the top of the cliff, with the cinematic camera dropping down the cliffside in order to show the audience its enormous height, reinforcing just how precarious Jesus' position had become. As the camera shot rises up to the top of the cliff once again, the notable escape has already happened, and Jesus is walking away from his would-be captors. The means of his escape goes unexplained, since the moment of his escape is conveniently spent showing the audience the ominous dangers of the cliffside.

These examples testify to the difficulties that storytellers have when narrating the events of Luke 4:28–30—difficulties that arise from the seemingly torturous relationship of the build-up of the incident's conflict and its resolution. But if the gap between Luke 4:28–29 and Luke 4:30 presents a puzzling picture of causality, it has attracted imaginative reconstruction in the novels of some recent storytellers. In an effort to explore the possible options for filling the "gap" between Luke 4:28–29 and Luke 4:30, consideration needs now to be given to the literary strategies employed by Jesus-novelists in their reconstruction of the Nazareth episode—a task to which we turn in the next chapter.

THREE

Navigating Strategies

Novel Imagination to the Rescue

HAVING NOTED THE CURIOUS way in which Luke narrates the plot of the Nazareth incident in Luke 4:28–30, our focus here shifts to exploring some of the strategies employed by various Jesus-novelists in their efforts to explicate the staging of the Lukan episode. Just as painters throughout history have imaginatively illuminated canonical episodes for the benefit of their viewers, so too Jesus-novelists imaginatively seek to illuminate canonical episodes for the benefit of their readers.[1] The Nazareth incident of Luke 4 has some traction in this enterprise. Attention to the recent "reception history" of the Nazareth incident (that is, how the text has been interpreted) will, of course, serve the purpose of illustrating the narrative "afterlife" that the Lukan passage has had. But more importantly, perhaps, it will also serve as a springboard for considering the broader theological contours of the Lukan narrative and how those contours might impact attempts to narrate the cause-and-effect relationships that are left unstated within the canonical account. And so, some of the strategies used to stage the curious depiction of Luke 4:28–30 appear in the following survey.

1. On the "visual exegesis" of Luke's Gospel, for example, see the three volumes by Hornik and Parsons in their series *Illuminating Luke* (vol. 1: *The Infancy Narrative*; vol. 2: *The Public Ministry of Christ*; vol. 3: *The Passion and Resurrection Narratives*).

Navigating Strategies

THE ATHLETIC DODGE

One strategy for enhancing the narrative of Luke 4:28–30 is what might be called "the athletic dodge." In this strategic approach to interpreting Luke 4:30, it is Jesus' extraordinary physical attributes that explain how it is that he escapes from the clutches of his townspeople.

This technique is best illustrated in the work of Walter Wangerin. The Nazareth incident from Luke's Gospel has attracted Wangerin's fictionalizing interests on not one but two occasions; first in his 1996 tome *The Book of God: The Bible as a Novel*, and then in his 2005 narrative *Jesus: A Novel*. Although the two accounts differ in some features, they both incorporate the athletic dodge, with Jesus ducking out from the maddened crowd and disappearing by means of his athletic prowess.

In the earlier of Wangerin's two versions (*The Book of God*), the Nazareth incident is not described by a nameless narrator but is recounted by Jesus' disciple Andrew (who was party to the incident) for the benefit of Simon Peter (one of Jesus' disciples who had not been involved). Andrew recounts the incident in this way:

> They couldn't stand it. Simon, I don't know how their anger changed from shouting to action—but soon the men had carried Jesus out of the synagogue and were driving him up the hill behind Nazareth. I ran to be with him. This was a mob. These people were enraged. They were forcing Jesus toward the edge of the hill. Simon, they planned to throw him over the cliff!
> But then Jesus grabbed my arm and pulled me sideways, and suddenly we were hidden in the bushes. He grinned and winked at me. "All my childhood I played in these hills," he said, and he led me away by another path.[2]

This imaginative recounting of the Nazareth episode proposes that, by means of his sheer athleticism and nimbleness, Jesus was able to jump out of the grip of the enraged crowd. And

---

2. Wangerin, *The Book of God*, 474.

more than that, while extracting himself from the crowd's grasp, Jesus managed also to drag Andrew along as well, saving him at the same time. Jesus' familiarity with the local area allowed him to know precisely when to jump into the nearby bushes, and gave him knowledge of the path system through which he made his escape, avoiding the crowd.

In the second of Wangerin's two versions (*Jesus: A Novel*), some of the narrative components differ. For instance, the episode is described by a narrator rather than being recounted by one of the characters who were involved in the incident. But Wangerin's second version of the Nazareth incident nonetheless shares the same general approach as his first version. It reads as follows, with Jesus still in the synagogue surrounded by angry townspeople:

> While the people were staggered and mute with fury, Jesus moved lightly through them and out the door.
> Then, for the second time that morning, the room erupted: howls of outrage. Men poured out the doors, a mob intent on driving this son of the Devil from their village, to the brow of a hill, to a bluff where they might pitch him headlong down—if they could find him.
> For, by a native mobility—athletic, light, and utterly confident—Mary's son had avoided them all and left the town on his own terms.[3]

Here again, as in Wangerin's earlier narration of the episode, Jesus is depicted as being able to outsmart others through his own lightness of foot and physical agility. Note, though, that in this version of the episode (unlike his first narration of it), the crowd seems never to have had Jesus in their grasp. From the canonical account in Luke 4:28–29, the crowd seems to have grabbed hold of Jesus and to be holding him at the edge of the cliff. But Wangerin does nothing with this in his second attempt to narrate the incident, presumably because the more one imagines the crowd getting Jesus close to the edge, the harder it is to

---

3. Wangerin, *Jesus*, 84–85.

narrate Jesus' escape in "realistic" terms. Wangerin's two versions of the Lukan episode differ, then, on this detail: whether Jesus was in the grip of the angry crowd or not. But both versions are consistent in depicting the outcome of the episode as being due to the fact that Jesus was agile, sprightly, and a touch sneaky.

The "athletic dodge" technique is also shared by Neil Boyd (whose 1984 book *The Hidden Years: A Novel about Jesus* is one of the best Jesus-novels to have been published in the second half of the twentieth century).[4] His narrative of the end of the Nazareth episode reads in this way:

> There was a tramp of feet and a crush of bodies as Jesus was separated from his weeping mother and carried up the hill, like a piece of wood on the tide. Their intention was never in doubt. They were going to rid their village of its shame once and for all.
>
> Jesus was pushed and jostled and poked up the narrow path he had taken so often on his nights of prayer. They were chanting a psalm to give them courage for the dreadful deed.
>
> At a bend in the path, he side-stepped smartly into one of the caves he had played in as a boy. He was on home ground.[5]

Virtually all the same ingredients that Wangerin utilizes are found already in Boyd's earlier, if underdeveloped, version.[6] The solution to Luke's puzzling narration is found in constructing

4. Boyd, *The Hidden Years*.

5. Ibid., 250. Another case in which the "athletic dodge" option may be evident is in O'Brien's novel *Theophilus*, 183: "They would have thrown him over to his death, but he slipped through them and walked away." Jesus avoids their grasp by adroitly "slipping through" them.

6. Boyd develops the incident further in a clever fashion. The Nazarenes had initially wondered whether they could lead Jesus to the cliffside without breaking the laws of Moses, since there is only so far that one can walk on the Sabbath without breaking the laws of the Sabbath. The rabbi assured them that the cliffside was within range. Jesus then escapes into the nearby caves. When he is finally found there, the lynching is foiled by the fact that the cave that he is in lies beyond the boundaries permitted for Sabbath walking (*The Hidden Years*, 250).

something of a sporty profile for Jesus. Neither Wangerin nor Boyd does much to develop this profile in episodes on either side of the Nazareth incident, but its utility in relation to the Nazareth incident offsets its lack of preceding build-up or subsequent development in their novels.[7]

THE MAGICAL MYSTERY MAN

Robert Graves's novel *King Jesus* represents another attempt to explain the curious Lukan climax by introducing new dimensions to Jesus' character. In his account of the Lukan Nazareth incident, Graves reads between the lines by heightening not Jesus' physical dexterity, as Wangerin and Boyd do, but by introducing readers to Jesus' magical prowess, like a great magical sorcerer of Hellenistic mythology. In a lengthy account, Graves fictionalizes the incident in this fashion.

> The officers of the synagogue were raging at these words and the six disciples began to fear for Jesus, Nazareth being notorious for its rough justice . . . [I]n Nazareth, as in many of the hill villages of Upper Galilee, the old ways were still followed. They called a cliff above the village the "Cliff of the Meddlers," and the tradition was that any person who preached dangerous new doctrine, meddled with magic, or claimed to be what he was not, must be toppled from it to his death.
>
> As soon as the service ended and Jesus came out of the synagogue, he was seized upon by the villagers and hustled up the hill. He calmly ordered his disciples: "Return to the house, my sons. Inform my mother that I will be with her presently."
>
> He did not struggle with his captors, but walked unconcernedly forward with them. Presently they released their hold of his arms because they found their fingers growing rigid with cramp. Jesus began to talk to them quietly about indifferent matters—the fruit crop, the

---

7. Kassoff (*The Book of Witnesses*, 41) narrates Jesus as one who was "quick and dexterous," but he does not develop this in relation to the Lukan Nazareth incident.

high price lately paid for a certain field through which they passed, the habits of the lapwing. Everyone fell silent as he talked, his voice growing louder and louder until it rose to a shot which rang in their ears and made the drums tingle, but then gradually died down to conversational tones again. They soon ceased to have any sense of what he was saying. Each man caught hold of his neighbour for support, and arm was linked in arm. His voice came to them in broken waves, like distant singing down the wind, as they continued drowsily up the hill. Nearer and nearer to the cliff they stumbled, every man asleep on his feet like an old mule in the shafts of a market cart.

Suddenly a loud cry rang through their ears: "Halt! Halt, Meddlers of Nazareth, or you are all dead men!"

They obeyed and stood in a long row, stupidly gazing down over the steep cliff-face. Another three steps and they would have perished. From a thicket on their right hand came the voice of Jesus again, ordering them to return in peace to their homes.

They turned and fled away in terror.[8]

Stripped from its narrative context in Graves's novel, this extract might be read as if it were meant to demonstrate Jesus' divine powers over those who would oppose him. But this is not its function within the larger narrative that Graves produces. Graves has no intention of depicting an "orthodox" portrait of Jesus, and his plotline steers clear of giving Jesus supernatural powers. Instead of Jesus' hypnotic effectiveness emerging from his (access to) supernatural power, the reader is to recognize Jesus as one who had amazing powers of persuasion, but not persuasive powers that outstrip the natural order of things. Graves amplifies the story of Jesus in ways that have no indebtedness to orthodox convictions about Jesus' relatedness to God. In fact, in Graves's storyline, Jesus is the natural son of Herod Archelaus and Mary, for instance, and his "miracles" were nothing out of the ordinary; instead, they were merely natural events that be-

8. Graves, *King Jesus*, 281–82.

came exaggerated in the process of storytelling and were later used illegitimately to demonstrate Jesus' ability to work supernatural miracles. Graves's novel attempts to show that such interpretations were wrong-headed amplifications, driven by eager but feeble-minded followers of Jesus.[9]

The same conviction dictates Graves's narration of the Nazareth incident. Rather than Jesus standing "in the place of others" (as in one theological interpretation of Jesus' crucifixion), here the Nazarenes stand in the place they had intended for Jesus—the cliff intended to deter meddlers. The event permits Jesus, the magical mystery man, to play a hypnotic trick on his persecutors through mind-bending sorcery. There is no macho athleticism here. Instead, Graves has shifted the episode into the genre of fantasy and sorcery, with Jesus conjuring up the resources of the hypnotist, the illusionist, the magician, in order to get himself out of a jam. For Graves, it is Jesus' mind-bending trickery that fills the gap of Luke 4:30.

JESUS HAD SYMPATHIZERS

Rather than enlarging the profile and characteristics of the central protagonist, another technique for fictionalizing the Lukan climax is to bring new characters to the scene. Those characters are then able to fill the gap in the Lukan narrative and alleviate its cause-and-effect oddities.

This strategy is evident in Bruce Chilton's book *Rabbi Jesus*. Chilton's book is a generic hybrid. It is a pseudo-narrative that sometimes reads like a novel and sometimes like an introductory academic text that provides the narrative sections with historical background. The Nazareth incident is not elaborated in a narrative section, but Chilton offers a gesture as to how he would

---

9. For instance, according to Graves (*King Jesus*, 292–96), Jesus' turning water into wine and feeding the 5,000 were simply occasions in which Jesus pretended to do these things; the people around him thought his play-acting was cute and decided to follow along with the spirit of things, pretending to benefit from his fictitious initiatives. This is indeed an imaginative interpretation.

have recounted the event when he writes: "Jesus must have had sympathizers in Nazareth, because he escaped."[10] Expanded into a fully-developed narrative, the account might involve some Nazarenes maneuvering themselves within the mob in order to encircle Jesus, progressively moving him to the periphery and, at an opportune time, jettisoning him from the mob—with all of this being unnoticed by the others in the mob. The envisaged scene makes for good drama and keeps the escape intact. It removes the oddity of the Lukan narrative by introducing new characters that step into the cause-and-effect breech that is gaping wide in the Gospel of Luke.

Something of this order is found in the novels by Marjorie Holmes and Nikos Kazantzakis. At nine pages, Holmes' narration of the Nazareth incident in her novel *The Messiah* is the most extended and developed of any of the examples considered here. In the climactic moment excerpted below, Jesus' grandmother is Hannah, his brothers are Josey (Joseph), Jude, Simon, and James, and local troublemakers include Ruben (a youth who had frequently pestered Jesus and his dog) and Abinadab (a member of the town council). The action here begins as the brothers of Jesus begin to strike back:

> Hannah felt herself shoved roughly aside from behind. "Get out of the way, Grandma," said James . . .
> Ruben floundered; he had time only to look over his shoulder before he was felled by the blow from Josey. He pitched forward, felt the hard ground, and smelled the bloody grass. He was vaguely aware that Jesus was being pulled to his feet by James. Two of the attackers tried to flee, but were caught by Jude and Simon and dragged back, to stand stubbornly defiant before the wrath of Mary's sons. The brothers had been tricked into a spurious debate inside [the synagogue], only racing to the scene when a frightened onlooker brought them word.

10. Chilton, *Rabbi Jesus*, 102.

"You beasts—you will pay dearly for this!" Josey raged, his round face livid, his small bright eyes ablaze. "If there's any justice in Nazareth, you will be punished."

"No, Josey, stop," Jesus ordered. He stood before them half naked, bruised and dirty from the ground; his battered nose was bleeding, one eye already swollen half shut. Blood also trickled from a corner of his mouth. He brushed the blood away impatiently with the back of his hand. "Forgive them. I forgive them, and so must you. They don't realize what they have done."

"But they should be arrested! They're brutes, they deserve it—this is wrong!"

Abinadab had been watching a safe distance away. Now he stalked up, pugnacious and self-righteous. "Why are you defending this imposter?" he demanded. "Why are you interfering?"

Josey wheeled on him, breathing hard, "Because he is our *brother!*"[11]

And with that, the episode pretty much finishes. There is no cliff hanging, and no concluding oddity. What we have instead is a demonstration of familial bonds rising above the onslaught of one's own kin.

In Kazantzakis' novel *The Last Temptation*, the Nazareth incident of Luke 4 is conflated with the account of Jesus' family seeking to remove him from the public eye because they perceive him to be something other than his normal self (Mark 3:31–35; Matt 12:46–50; Luke 8:19–21). One thing leads to another, and before long there is all-out mayhem, with Jesus' followers, and even his family, fighting against the local townspeople who, we're told, had "become rabid," so that they were in a mood for "murdering each other." Judas wields a dagger to keep the townspeople away from Jesus, eventually tossing one Nazarene to the ground and putting the dagger to the man's throat. Philip blindly swings his staff in the air, threatening the crowd. And Peter is shown to hold "a huge heavy stone" that he crashes down onto the foot of

---

11. Holmes, *The Messiah*, 134–35.

Navigating Strategies

one of the old men of the village, crushing the foot in the process. Just then, the rabbi of the synagogue appears. He is Simeon, one of Jesus' uncles. So we read:

> [A]t that moment the rabbi appeared, panting. He had heard the uproar and had jumped up from his table . . . and ran to see what was happening. He had encountered several of the wounded along the way and learnt everything. He now pushed aside the crowd and reached the son of Mary. [He rebuked Jesus for preaching love but stirring up hatred, and then . . .] He turned to the crowd: "My children, return to your homes. This is my nephew. He's sick, unfortunate man; he's been sick for years. Do not bear any malice against him for what he has said, but forgive him. It is not he who speaks, but someone else who uses his mouth."
> "God!" Jesus exclaimed.
> "You keep quiet," the rabbi snapped . . . He turned once more to the crowd: "Leave him alone, my children. Bear no grudge against him, for he knows not what he says. All—rich and poor—we are all seeds of Abraham. Do not quarrel amongst yourselves. It's noontime, return to your homes. I shall cure this unfortunate man" . . .
> The square . . . emptied . . .
> "Come, fellow-partisans," said Jesus, "let us go. Shake the dust from your feet. Farewell, Nazareth!"
> "I'll keep you company until the edge of the village so that no one bothers you," the old rabbi said.
> He took Jesus' hand and they went in the lead together.[12]

Although Kazantzakis has a troupe of Jesus' disciples actively involved in deterring the maddened crowd, the rescue is effected solely by one rescuer—the influential respected local rabbi of Jesus' own kin. But whether the rescue is imagined to be set in motion by a group of local Nazarenes who come to Jesus' aid (as in Chilton and Holmes) or by a single figure (as in Kazantzakis), for these authors cause-and-effect linkage in the

---

12. Kazantzakis, *The Last Temptation*, 353–60.

Nazareth incident is dramatized solely in relation to human relations, without remainder. As a consequence, the curious oddity of the Lukan conclusion is erased altogether.

THE REWRITTEN ENDING

The three strategies noted above all make adjustments in one way or another to the Lukan storyline in order to bring an element of narrative satisfaction to the Lukan Nazareth incident. They introduce adjustments to the story by tinkering primarily with the episode's characterization, either by adding resources to the protagonist's personality or by adding new characters to the narration.

Another form of tinkering takes place primarily in relation to the episode's plot, rather than its characterization.[13] This tendency is evident, for instance, in Jeffrey Archer's 2007 novel *The Gospel according to Judas, by Benjamin Iscariot*. The episode is simply recounted. When Jesus claims "Today, this scripture has been fulfilled in your hearing," three sentences conclude the episode:[14] "One or two of the Pharisees murmured among themselves: Is this not Joseph's son? Jesus answered: A prophet is never without fame, except in his own country. Others, who still wanted to believe, continued to ask: Who is this man?"

Here, the conflict of the Lukan original is maintained, but only minimally. The number of those who take offence at Jesus is reduced dramatically (i.e., only "one or two of the Pharisees"),

---

13. At times this distinction between adjustments to characterization, on the one hand, and adjustments to plot, on the other hand, is admittedly somewhat fluid (as in the case of Marcus Harrison's novel, considered below), but there is generally merit in positing the distinction.

14. Archer, *The Gospel according to Judas, by Benjamin Iscariot*, 11. Archer's abbreviated storyline is not due to an indebtedness to Mark's account in Mark 6:1–6. While the saying about the prophet being without honor appears in both Mark (6:4) and Luke (4:24), all other points of contact between Archer's scene and the biblical text are with Luke's account: Jesus' claim "today . . ." (Luke 4:21), and the description of Jesus as "Joseph's son" (Luke 4:22; contra "Mary's son" of Mark 6:3).

Navigating Strategies

and nothing is done to act on the offence, other than simply to murmur against him. Archer's account significantly reduces the conflict between Jesus and his townspeople to a bit of tension between Jesus and two Pharisees. Moreover, he qualifies the minimal tension of the incident by noting that, in fact, some of the people of Nazareth actually "wanted to believe" in Jesus.[15] Evidently, then, when narrating his version of the Lukan Nazareth incident, Archer felt little constraint from the account in Luke 4:28-30.

Other modern novelists also sidestep the odd ending of the Lukan episode, although they often manage to keep the conflict between Jesus and the townspeople intact. One simple example of conflict without oddity is found in David Kassoff's novel *The Book of Witnesses*:[16] "He [Jesus] spoke in the synagogue, on the Sabbath. He read from some of the prophecies of Isaiah and then made the lesson sound as though the prophecies referred to *him!* Caused a commotion . . . The people got very angry indeed. They ran him out of town." This is clean narration, with some dramatic conflict and a conclusion that is sequenced without extraordinary elements. The conflict between the characters remains, but the odd Lukan climax is wholly by-passed in this fictionalization. There is no cliff-clawing going on, and no stunning escape. The bizarre Lukan climax is compromised in order to achieve a certain narrative consistency and believability.

Pride of place for the rewritten plot must go to Marcus Harrison's novel, *The Memoirs of Jesus Christ*, published in 1975.[17]

---

15. Archer also removes any mention of Nazareth from his account. For Archer, the point is that a prophet is "without honour except in his own *country*" (*The Gospel according to Judas, by Benjamin Iscariot*, 11).

16. Kassoff, *The Book of Witnesses*, 70. The same ending appears twice in Gompertz's *A Jewish Novel about Jesus*, where Jesus is said to have been "run out of town" (70) and "rejected" (78) at Nazareth, but where there is no mention of them intending to stone him.

17. Harrison, *The Memoirs of Jesus Christ*, 149. I am leaving to one side Norman Mailer's handling of the incident, in which Jesus himself (writing to set the record straight) knows of Luke's account and assesses it to be a deficient case of anti-Semitism. The issue of potential tendencies toward anti-Semitism

According to the plotline of this book, these "memoirs" are written by Jesus himself after the destruction of Jerusalem in 70 CE. Now an old man, Jesus has been hiding away in a monastery for many years after his supposed death on a Roman cross decades earlier. In these memoirs, this elderly Jesus tries to set the record straight, trying to undermine the movement that has begun in his name and that has been bolstered by the fallacious Gospels of Matthew, Mark, Luke, and John. Within this context, the Nazareth incident is recounted by Jesus in this fashion: "The crowd muttered, 'Stone him!' . . . As I reached the door, John opened it while Peter, Andrew, and Judas stepped between me and the mob. Peter drew his sword and waved it crying ferociously, 'Back! Back!' He advanced and the mob faltered. Judas and Andrew hustled me through the door; when we were all outside, Peter joined us and we barred the door against them. There were planks of timber lying about and we piled them up to make an obstacle."

At this point, Jesus and his disciples remember that their ["our"] women were upstairs in the synagogue's gallery reserved for women and children. So Jesus and his disciples re-enter the synagogue, run up to the gallery and grab the women, escorting them through the mob in the synagogue. The episode ends with this sentence: "We ran downstairs and piled more timber against the door, then mounted up [on our horses] and rode out of Nazareth."[18]

This is exciting stuff, without a narrative oddity in sight, except, of course, for those cognizant of the canonical storyline. For them, it might be tremendously bizarre to hear about Jesus and his disciples mounting onto speeding horses in a mad dash to extract themselves from danger. But scenes such as this are not out of place in the Harrison novel, which depicts Jesus as the

---

in the canonical Gospels is an important issue but one that cannot be dealt with here. In a sense, though, Mailer's narrative might be regarded as a type of rewritten-ending Jesus-novels, since Jesus offers a storyline that differs from Luke's at the point of the episode's conclusion.

18. Harrison, *The Memoirs of Jesus Christ*, 149.

Navigating Strategies

well-placed son of an elite and powerful man, a Jesus who bears little relation to the Jesus of the Gospels. Evidently, when there's enormous wealth within the family, well-bred hurtling horses are nothing out of the ordinary.

In Harrison's attempt at fictionalizing the Lukan storyline, then, Jesus escapes not through his own nimbleness, as in Wangerin and Boyd, nor through weaving a hypnotic trance on his abductors, as in Graves. Nor are the Nazarenes pacified by their leading rabbi, as in Kazantzakis, or tricked by sympathizers of Jesus, as in Chilton, or beaten back by the brothers of Jesus, as in Holmes. Nor do the people of Nazareth simply run him out of town, as in Kassoff. There is an escape here, as in Luke, but the odd feature of the Lukan escape is replaced by the protagonist's blockading of a door and a dazzling charge of stampeding horses. Here, Nazareth has been visited by someone akin to a sandaled Indiana Jones.

◆ ◆ ◆

We have taken note of four common strategies that allow Jesus-novelists to iron out Luke's curious climax of the Nazareth incident in Luke 4:30: (1) the athletic dodge; (2) Jesus the magical mystery man; (3) Jesus gets assistance from sympathizers; and (4) the rewritten ending. At this point, it will serve us well to consider whether the theological commitments evident within the Lukan narratives of the Gospel of Luke and the Acts of the Apostles might suggest that yet another strategy should be added to the interpretive options—a matter to which we now turn.

FOUR

Discovering Patterns
Luke 4:30 and Divine Causality

KNOWING WHAT TO LOOK FOR

CHRISTIAN SMITH, A SOCIOLOGIST of religion and culture, has recently stated that when he and other sociologists try to explain lines of cause-and-effect relationship, "we have to know what we are looking for, how to look for it, and what it is like when we see causes at work producing results."[1] Smith is talking about cause-and-effect relationships within what we might call "the natural world," but his comment might well have relevance to issues of cause-and-effect relationships as depicted in the Lukan narratives. Those narratives demonstrate that "knowing what we are looking for" has everything to do with the ability to see "causes at work producing results" in a way that is aligned with knowing "how to look" for them.

As we have seen in chapter 3, the sizeable narrative gap of Luke 4:30 allows novelists to exercise imaginative muscle in their attempts to explain Jesus' release from the grip of the maddened crowd. But while their attempts rate high on the scale of imaginative proficiency, they need also to be critiqued by the narrative's own literary and theological configuration, which itself guides

---

1. Smith, "Five Proposals for Reforming Article Publishing," 592.

Discovering Patterns

the audience in terms of knowing "what to look for" and "how to look for it."

It has been popular to imagine that a literary text is simply a blank slate upon which readers impose their own interests in a search to bring meaning where there is otherwise virtually nothing.[2] But the tide of opinion is turning on this matter, it seems to me, back to a more nuanced view of things. It is true, of course, that the various ingredients of one's location and identity impacts on one's reading assumptions and strategies. But it also seems to be the case that the text itself contributes to the reading process, with aspects of the text needing to be negotiated in capable readings.

The point is pertinent especially with regard to the process of finding and filling gaps within the narrative. In his book *The Poetics of Biblical Narrative*, for instance, Robert Funk argued that texts inherently guide their audience so that, through cognizance of "various markers and signals in the text," the audience inevitably "discovers patterns, supplies what is felt to be missing, [and] constructs plot, character, and the like."[3] In a book that shares the same title (*The Poetics of Biblical Narrative*), Meir Sternberg stated the following:

> To emphasize the active role played by the reader in constructing the world of a literary work is by no means to imply that gap-filling is an arbitrary process. On the contrary, in this as in other operations of reading, literature is remarkable for its powers of control and validation. Of course, gap-filling may nevertheless be performed in a wild or misguided or tendentious fashion, and there is no lack of evidence for this in criticism ancient or modern. But *to gain cogency*, a hypothesis must be legitimated by the text.[4]

---

2. See, for example, Fish, *Is There a Text in This Class?*; Tompkins, *Reader-Response Criticism*; Mailloux, *Interpretive Conventions*; Flynn and Schweickart, *Gender and Reading*; Freund, *The Return of the Reader*.

3. Funk, *The Poetics of Biblical Narrative*, 36.

4. Sternberg, *The Poetics of Biblical Narrative*, 188, emphasis added.

Hearing the Silence

Compare also Kavin Rowe's discussion of what happens when audiences encounter literary gaps:

> Certain strands of literary theory of the last twenty or thirty years have made much of such gaps or silences. The focus . . . has usually been on the reader's role in filling the gap. That the reader is involved in the reading process at the point of filling in gaps and silences is beyond question. But it does not follow that all gap-filling is entirely and only subjectively constructed interpretation, located arbitrarily . . . and solely in the mind of the reader, or in the strategies of the community. Rather . . . a text itself has certain norms and directives, and in order for an interpretation to gain plausibility, it must be legitimated by the text's own norms. No interpretation can claim cogency, therefore, if it clashes with some of the givens of the text, or fills in what the text itself rules out, or ignores textual particulars, for example. Instead, the success of gap-filling as a hermeneutical process depends on its "congruity" with the text's own norms and directives.[5]

These quotations have been cited expansively precisely because they make points that cannot be jettisoned when considering the full dynamics of textual interpretation. In a hermeneutical circle in which the auditor engages with a text in ever-improved cycles of understanding about the text's "various markers and signals," the narrative itself sets up parameters regarding the live interpretive options an audience might entertain in its quest to appreciate the full dimensions of a narrative gap. The process whereby an audience makes efforts to construct connective structures when seeking to assimilate the fullness of a text's potential is described by Wolfgang Iser in this way: "we look forward, we look back, we decide, we change our decisions, we form expectations, we are shocked by their nonfulfillment, we question, we muse, we accept, we reject."[6] Accordingly, "[A]s the reading experience is en-

---

5. Rowe, *Early Narrative Christology*, 37–38.
6. Iser, "The Reading Process," 293.

Discovering Patterns

acted, and as horizons [within a text] appear and disappear, the reader strives to create 'coherence' out of the disparate, mutating, fleeting moments of reading, ... [always] practicing 'consistency building.'"[7]

In this light, it is telling that not one of the four narrative strategies outlined in chapter 3 arise naturally from the "givens" and "particulars" of the Lukan narratives—their "norms and directives." There is nothing in the Lukan narratives to suggest that Jesus was a nimble athlete; that might have been the case, of course, but Luke's texts do not register impressions of Jesus' athletic ability one way or the other. Similarly, there is nothing in the Lukan narratives to suggest that Jesus was simply an ordinary man with incredible hypnotic powers; Luke's texts go out of their way to counter perceptions of Jesus that imagine him to be anything less than "both Lord and Messiah" (Acts 2:36). For the same reason, there is nothing in the Lukan narratives to suggest that Jesus was the son of an elite man with resources that enabled his escape. And with regard to his having a cohort of sympathizers who could assist his get-away, the Lukan narrative would seem to work against that possibility. In Luke's Gospel, the Nazareth incident takes place before he calls any disciples to accompany him, and it makes clear that "all in the synagogue were filled with rage" (4:28). If the Lukan narratives allow certain interpretive possibilities and rule out others, each of the four possibilities already considered in chapter 3 would seem not to be animated by (and in some cases seem to run contrary to) the "norms and directives" of the Lukan texts. As such, they have little claim to be "plausible" or "legitimate" options when judged by "the givens of the text." Of course, a Jesus-novelist has every right to move beyond the confines of the canonical text—and, as we have seen, some relish the chance to challenge canonical texts at as many points as possible. But searching for a gap-filling interpretation

---

7. This is the description of Iser's position offered by "The Bible and Culture Collective" in *The Postmodern Bible*, 32.

of Luke 4:30 that is "congruous" within the contours of the Lukan narratives requires us to look beyond such imaginative strategies.

PROPOSING A CONGRUOUS FILLER

In the remainder of this chapter and the following chapter, I want to propose and elaborate a different interpretive possibility for Luke 4:30. That is, I want to suggest that this "under-narrated" verse flows somewhat disjointedly from within its narrative context precisely in order to grab the audience's attention for the purposes of challenging and enhancing the audience's reading strategy. The proposal involves three primary points:

1. The yawning gap in the narration of Luke 4:30 is like a clue embedded within the text that begs the audience to pick up on it and to develop it in ways consonant with larger patterns, emphases, and configurations within the text.
2. In particular, the gap of Luke 4:30 is to be filled with divine involvement and causality, rather than human cause-and-effect relationships.
3. This interpretation has cogency precisely because it does not clash with "the text's own norms and directives" but is, in fact, wholly congruent with them—both literarily (i.e., Lukan rhetorical techniques) and theologically.

In this proposal, the highly curious narrative of Luke 4:30 springs from and enriches a theological strand that pervades the Lukan narratives from start to finish—a theological conviction that, in fact, has the potential to short-circuit the standard canons of storytelling. The narrative of Luke 4:30 is not meant as an occasion to explore impressively creative means for Jesus to escape from the clutches of his townspeople by extraordinary physical dexterity or by overwhelming mental powers or by an alliance of colleagues or by hyper-charged horses. Instead, Luke 4:30 may be gaping wide in its explication of cause-and-effect relationships precisely in order to force the reader to give consideration to a different kind of cause-and-effect relationship, one that emerges frequently from the pages of the Lukan narrative, and one involving divine initiative within the course of events.[8]

This proposal—that an unstated divine initiative is in play— is not original to me, of course. As long ago as 1896, for instance, Alfred Plummer suggested that "there was something miraculous in [Jesus'] passing through the very midst of those who were intending to slay Him."[9] I have no reason to believe that the suggestion was original even to Plummer. But the proposal seems to merit stronger consideration than has generally been the case in scholarly discourse. Outlining those merits is the task at hand here and in subsequent chapters.

It is, of course, true that the text of Luke 4 "gives no indication of whether [Jesus passing through the midst of his oppressors was] miraculous or not."[10] But even if there are no *explicit* indications of this, it would nonetheless be a mistake to assume that a miraculous intervention should be excluded as an interpretive possibility for explaining the lines of causality in Luke 4:30, especially when that passage is set against the backdrop of the Lukan worldview, as reconstructed from a broader engagement with the Lukan narratives. In this regard, notice Sternberg's description of how a reader assesses possibilities for interpreting a text:

> To understand a literary work, we have to answer, in the course of reading, a series of such questions as: What is happening or has happened, and why? What connects the present event or situation to what went before, and how do both relate to what will probably come after?

---

8. On this theme, see further Gaventa, "Initiatives Divine and Human in the Lukan Story World."

9. Plummer, *A Critical and Exegetical Commentary on the Gospel according to S. Luke*, 130. Plummer was wrong to imagine that this implication can be picked up from the phrase "passing through their midst" in Luke 4:30. Instead, the implication derives from a much more nuanced reading strategy, as set out in this book.

10. Culy et al., *Luke*, 142.

> ... And what norms govern the existence and conduct of all [the characters]? It is the set of answers given that enables the reader to reconstruct the field of reality devised by the text, to make sense of the represented world.[11]

To answer what is happening at any given point, a reader needs to know not only what has happened and what might come after, but also needs to be cognizant of the "norms" that "govern the existence" of the characters in order to "reconstruct the field of reality" or the worldview that undergirds the storyline; informed by the structures and ethos of that "represented world," the reader is better prepared to engage in an analysis of "what is happening" at any given point in a text, especially when negotiating sizeable narrative gaps in that text.

The dimension of the Lukan "field of reality" that is most pertinent to the consideration of Luke 4:30 is the conviction that the story of Jesus and his followers is shot through with insuperable divine involvement. While this is obviously the case in Luke's Gospel, it is also evident in the narratives of the Acts of the Apostles, where divine involvement is emphasized again and again. The narrative of Luke's second volume illustrates repeatedly that, when the story of salvation appears to come to a dead-end, when everything that seems to be of God appears to be in peril, when all hope in God's ongoing triumph is lost, when the gospel appears to be obstructed by the initiatives of those who would stand against it—precisely in those instances, and often in the face of personal tragedy and loss, the divine initiative flows, energizing new initiatives, often in surprising and inscrutable ways, in order to accomplish the remarkable and the otherwise unachievable.[12]

The fact that this appears to be one of the most conspicuous of Luke's theological convictions should cause us to consider

---

11. Sternberg, *The Poetics of Biblical Narrative*, 186.

12. This dimension of Lukan narrative theology is explored against the backdrop of the destruction of Jerusalem and its temple by the forces of Rome in Longenecker, "Rome's Victory and God's Honour."

Discovering Patterns

whether it comes into play in the curious happening recounted in Luke 4:30. Does the narrative there resonate with motifs elsewhere in the Lukan writings? Charles Talbert puts things this way: "The escape of Jesus (4:30) foreshadows the story in Acts where the gospel triumphantly survived similar acts of hostility and rejection."[13] As the Acts narrative repeatedly demonstrates, the survival of the gospel could not have been achieved apart from divine involvement in overcoming hostility and rejection.[14] Perhaps, then, Luke 4:30 needs also to be considered in relation to *divine* involvement of some fashion.

This possibility has further merit when Luke 4:30 is compared not only to the narrative of Acts but also to an episode recounted late in Luke's Gospel itself. The point is intimated by Scott Cunningham, who links Luke 4:30 not only to the Acts narrative but to the Easter event itself: "With this cryptic statement [Luke 4:30] Luke introduces a theme that will recur repeatedly

---

13. Talbert, *Reading Luke*, 57. On this theme, see especially Squires, *The Plan of God in Luke-Acts*. According to Squires, the theme of God's insuperable plan "is one of the means by which Luke attempted to integrate his narrative [i.e., both Luke's Gospel and the Acts of the Apostles] and present his story in a cohesive manner" (186).

14. The relationship of Luke's Gospel to the Acts of the Apostles needs here to be discussed, albeit briefly. In my view, (1) Luke wrote his Gospel in the expectation that he would later write a history that highlighted events pertaining to the rise of the early-Jesus movement (i.e., the Acts of the Apostles), and (2) that knowledge allowed him to shape his Gospel in certain ways in the light of what would transpire in the narrative of Acts. I suspect Luke fully expected that his Gospel would be read without knowledge of Acts (and perhaps even vice versa), and this would not have caused him any angst; in fact, he probably circulated his Gospel years prior to the circulation of Acts. But I also suppose that, for him, the best readings of either text would arise out of knowledge of how the one volume related to the other. This is virtually implied in his opening sentence of Acts: "In the first book, Theophilus, I wrote about . . ." For more, see Longenecker, *Rhetoric at the Boundaries*, 215–26. Schnelle's comments (*Theology of the New Testament*, 463) are largely on track but are slightly too inflexible when he writes: "Luke understands [his Gospel] and Acts as a narrative unity, to be read and understood as a whole, a unified historical composition, so that any adequate interpretation must be based on both writings." For recent discussion on the matter, see Gregory and Rowe, *Rethinking the Unity and Reception of Luke and Acts*.

[throughout his writings]. Nothing can stop the progress of the spread of the Word of God. In some respects, this incident foreshadows the Easter event, but it should also be seen as prefiguring the frequent escapes from persecution by the disciples in Acts."[15]

That the Nazareth incident "foreshadows the Easter event" can be demonstrated by the close resemblances that the Nazareth incident shares with the account of Jesus' death and resurrection. In both, Jesus is accosted; in both, his assailants want him to be removed from the scene; in both, they attempt to orchestrate his death; and in both, his accosters do not ultimately get their way. Of course there is a fundamental difference between the two episodes, since obviously Jesus does not die in the first episode. But the two incidents share features similar enough to see a close literary connection between them. As I. Howard Marshall notes, "various commentators see an anticipation of the passion and resurrection" in the Lukan Nazareth incident.[16] The view that the Nazareth incident is a presage to the crucifixion-Easter narratives is not unfounded, since similar characteristics are exhibited by the two Lukan episodes.

If it is right to recognize a literary relationship between Luke's accounts of the Nazareth incident and of Jesus' death and resurrection, it is also likely that the Lukan audience is to envision similar lines of causality to be operating within those two accounts. Whereas it is clearly divine initiative that results in the resurrection of Jesus, so too it must be divine initiative that results in Jesus becoming disentangled from the brutal crowd, walking through the midst of the Nazarenes, and going on his way.

Perhaps this way of understanding the unnarrated causality within Luke 4:30 would have arisen for the audience not so much on its initial encounter with the Lukan Gospel but only

---

15. Cunningham, *Through Many Tribulations*, 65.

16. Marshall, *The Gospel of Luke*, 190. See, for instance, Schürmann, *Das Lukasevangelium*, vol. 1, 240–41; Moessner, "Reading Luke's Gospel as Ancient Hellenistic Narrative," 138–39.

Discovering Patterns

in subsequent encounters, as the story took root in their minds and their ability to make connections would have grown and developed. This is not surprising or unusual; instead, it is precisely how audiences inevitably engage with narrative texts (along with other kinds of texts)—not least, in the ancient world of oral delivery and aural reception.[17] For instance, in her work on Mark's Gospel, Elizabeth Struthers Malbon makes the point this way: "I do not claim that a first reader or a first hearer would observe all that I have suggested here . . . Yet I do assume that Mark's first hearers probably heard more as listeners to an oral narration than we do. And I have no reason to assume that Mark expected his narrative to have only one hearing or one reading. In fact, the implied reader of Mark would appear to be a rereader!"[18]

Associating the Nazareth incident and the death and resurrection of Jesus gives this "reading-through-rereading" a rhetorical advantage over interpretations of Luke 4:30 that do not include divine involvement. The proposed association enables the audience to perceive Jesus' public ministry as being encased (in a sense) between these two incidents—incidents that, pre-

---

17. When defending his interpretation of Paul, Douglas Campbell makes a related point regarding the non-narratival text of Romans ("An Attempt to be Understood," forthcoming, emphasis added): "[S]ome of my critics seem to suppose that Paul's letter to the Romans was meant to be comprehensible on one reading, like a modern English text . . . But this concern betrays an anachronism. Ancient texts were difficult syllabic documents lacking a vast amount of interpretative assistance delivered to modern readers by way of punctuation. They were so different from modern texts that they had to be read repeatedly, and practically memorized, before being read out loud more definitively. And *then they were often reread and pressed for further insights*."

18. Malbon, "Echoes and Foreshadowings in Mark 4–8, 228. She continues (ibid., 229–30): "The implied author does not expect the disciples to understand the good news of Jesus Christ, Son of God, until it has been fully told, from baptism through resurrection, and fully heard—and heard again. The same expectation applies to the implied reader . . . The disciples are to rehear; the implied reader is to reread . . . Both disciples and readers are called to be rehearers/rereaders. Both are asked to perceive that messiahs are not always what they seem at first glance." See further Beavis, "The Trial before the Sanhedrin."

cisely in their literary resemblances, highlight the surprising ways in which God often chooses to act in the world. Whereas the Nazareth incident is the first specific incident of Jesus' public ministry recounted in the Lukan narrative,[19] his death and resurrection appear at the conclusion of Jesus' public ministry. Together, then, these two accounts form an *inclusio*—a literary device that marks out a section of material at its beginning and end, like bookends on a shelf that keep the books between them together.

Literary techniques of this sort lie wholly within the rhetorical expertise of a storyteller of Luke's caliber. In fact, as I have pointed out elsewhere, Paul's apostolic ministry is recounted in Acts in much the same fashion, with a particular structural marker (which I call "chain-link construction") appearing at the start and finish of Luke's account of Paul's apostolic endeavors in planting Jesus-communities around the Mediterranean basin— the chain-link structure serving, in a sense, as two bookends that help to contain a single major text unit.[20] Perhaps a similar concern to "bookend" Jesus' public ministry links the Nazareth episode and the resurrection narrative. As two parts of a literary *inclusio*, each episode resembles the other in sustaining the conviction that, when Jesus is caught in the grip of death, the surprising initiative of God enters the narrative frame in some fashion.

---

19. Luke sets the stage for this incident in Luke 4:14–15, where he recounts that Jesus had begun to teach in synagogues and had been praised by everyone. But Luke gives priority to the Nazareth incident as the key moment in which Jesus' public ministry becomes defined (not least in relation to an Isaianic matrix), and thereby inaugurated. Prior to the Nazareth incident, we hear nothing from Jesus himself during this preliminary stage of his public ministry, and only at the Nazareth incident do we hear Jesus pronounce, "Today this scripture has been fulfilled in your hearing" (4:21).

20. See Longenecker, *Rhetoric at the Boundaries*, 171–92, 198–205, and 231, where Paul's public ministry of planting communities of Jesus-followers in Acts 13–19 is shown to be marked out at the start and the finish by a "chain-link" construction, facilitating an *inclusio* around that period of Paul's life.

Discovering Patterns

This linking of the first and last main episodes of Jesus' public ministry has not been lost on Jesus-novelists. Marjorie Holmes, for instance, captures precisely this link in her narrating of the Nazareth incident when she has Jesus instruct his brother Joses in this way: "Forgive them . . . They don't realize what they have done." Foreshadowing Jesus' later words from the cross ("Father forgive them, for they don't know what they are doing"; Luke 23:34), Holmes links the lynching of the Nazareth incident to the lynching of Jesus at his crucifixion.[21] Maintaining this arc from Luke 4 to the end of the Lukan Gospel simply requires the reader to spot the implicit correspondence between (1) Jesus' release from the death-intent grip of the Nazareth townspeople and (2) Jesus' release from the grip of death in his resurrection.

This way of interpreting Luke 4:28–30 has implications regarding imaginative reconstructions of the ending of the Nazareth incident. When that incident is read in relation to the narrative of Jesus' death and resurrection, the yawning cavern evident in the cause-and-effect relationships of Luke 4:30 comes to be seen in a new light. No longer is it seen to be a surprising or embarrassing literary problem that needs to be resolved by postulating imaginative solutions regarding human efforts to release Jesus from the grip of the Nazareth townspeople. The wise and informed reader (or "rereader") of Luke's Gospel is evidently to imagine cause-and-effect relationships of an altogether different kind when exploring possible narrations for the otherwise curious events of Luke 4:30. The curiosity that arises from the under-narration of those events helps to crystallize the theological perspective that is fundamental to the Lukan narrative:

---

21. Holmes is not to know that Jesus' words from the cross "Father forgive them" is most likely a later scribal insertion into Luke's Gospel. See Omanson, *A Textual Guide to the Greek New Testament*, 152. He notes that although the saying "is probably not a part of the original Gospel of Luke . . . it may well be an authentic saying of Jesus" from the cross. Whitlark and Parsons ("The 'Seven' Last Words") propose that "Father forgive them" was added to Luke's Gospel in order to give seven-fold "completion" to Jesus' final words from the cross in canonical perspective.

Wherever God is active, insuperable obstacles are overcome, often in ways peculiar and surprising.[22] The narrative grounding for this conviction is found primarily in the events of Jesus' death and resurrection, which themselves are prefigured in the Nazareth events recounted in Luke 4:28-30. Accordingly, the Lukan Nazareth incident can be seen to offer a sleek and miniature version of the reality-defining events of the death and resurrection of Jesus, in which cause-and-effect relationships bypass the normal course of human involvement and are explainable by divine initiative alone.

THE THEOLOGICAL NECESSITY OF DIVINE DELIVERANCE

The prospect that divine causality resides within the literary gap of Luke 4:30 has pertinence not only to the Lukan theology of divine initiative but also to Luke's presentation regarding the death of Jesus and the particular "configuration" that Luke gives to that event.

Of relevance here is the "journey motif" that marks out the middle chapters of the Lukan Gospel, where Jesus devotes his energies to making his way to Jerusalem in order to undergo death there (i.e., 9:51-53, 57; 10:38; 13:31-33; 17:11; 19:28). As Jesus himself declares while on that journey, his impending death simply cannot bypass the city of Jerusalem but must be orchestrated within the city itself. So he takes his twelve disciples aside and explains to them, "See, we are going up to Jerusalem (ἀναβαίνομεν

---

22. It is interesting (but not instructive) to compare one part of the apocryphal story of Jesus (or "Issa") during his "hidden years." The account of "the Life of Issa" postulates that Jesus spent seventeen years of his life (from thirteen to twenty-nine years of age) in India, learning Buddhism and Hinduism. In that wholly contrived text, we read of one incident when "Issa" chastises the leading men of an Indian region: "After having listened to him, the magi determined to do him no harm. But at night, when all the town lay sleeping, they conducted him outside of the walls and abandoned him on the high road, in the hope that he would soon become a prey to the wild beasts. But, protected by the Lord our God, Saint Issa continued his way unmolested" (8.23-24).

Discovering Patterns

εἰς Ἰερουσαλήμ), and everything that is written about the Son of Man by the prophets will be accomplished" (Luke 18:31). In Luke's reconstruction of things, a "scriptural constraint" informs and restricts the ministry of Jesus, to the extent that a christological fulfillment of Scripture ensures and requires that his death take place in Jerusalem.

Much the same is evident in another of Jesus' statements in Luke's Gospel: "I must be on my way (δεῖ με ... πορεύεσθαι)," he says, "because it is impossible for a prophet to be killed outside of Jerusalem" (Luke 13:33).[23] The verb "to be on one's way" (πορεύεσθαι) that appears in this saying is an important one in Luke's Gospel, being spread throughout the central travel narrative of Luke 9:51—19:10 (9:51, 57; 10:38; 17:11; 19:28, 36), where Luke's theological interests are especially prominent. And notably, the same verb appears also in the conclusion of the Nazareth incident in Luke 4:30, usually translated "and he went on his way." That this verb in Luke 4:30 resonates with Luke's prominent travel narrative is a view articulated by Joseph Fitzmyer. According to him, the verb in Luke 4:30 is "the first occurrence of the significant verb *poreuesthai* in the Gospel proper" and thereby carries the nuances of Jesus being "on his way—a way that will eventually lead him to Jerusalem, the city of destiny."[24] Quite simply, for Jesus to have died anywhere except Jerusalem is a theological impossibility in Luke's Gospel. Jesus reinforces the point on the final night of his life, when he says to his disciples, "The Son of Man is going (πορεύεται) as it has been determined" (Luke 22:22).

---

23. On the issues pertaining to this verse, see especially Fisk, "See my Tears." Fisk writes: "Not only is the roll call of prophets martyred in Jerusalem surprisingly short, but there are obvious counterexamples . . . Simply put rejected prophets were *not* routinely brought to Jerusalem for trial and execution . . . Jesus' quest to reach *and die in* Jerusalem conforms to no known pattern" (155).

24. Fitzmyer, *The Gospel according to Luke*, vol. 1, 539; the earlier uses of πορεύομαι in Luke's Gospel (1:6, 39; 2:3, 41) fall outside of what Fitzmyer calls the "Gospel proper."

Luke's Gospel articulates yet another reason why divine necessity prevents Jesus' life from ending at the bottom of a Nazareth cliff. As Jesus says in Luke 4:43, it is necessary for him to preach the good news of the kingdom of God "to the other cities also; for I was sent for this purpose." The point for our purposes is obvious: Jesus' ministry was divinely configured in such a fashion that a Nazareth cliff would not be the place of his death.

That Luke 4:43 is significant to the thesis of this chapter is evidenced further by the structural relationship of that verse to the Nazareth incident itself. The claim that Jesus was sent to preach to other cities also appears at the end of the text-unit that the Nazareth incident inaugurates (i.e., Luke 4:14–44), and can be seen as playing off that incident. The material within Luke 4:14–44 falls within two main sections, each contained within an *inclusio* at 4:14–15 and 4:44—two summary statements about Jesus' ministry in synagogues. Between these two summarizing "inclusion points" stand (1) the Nazareth incident of 4:16–30, which serves to characterize the teaching of Jesus, and (2) the various healings and exorcisms of 4:31–41/42, which serve to characterize the powerful work of Jesus. At the end of each of these two sections, the ministry of Jesus is threatened—either by the murderous Nazarene mob of who would kill him if they had their way, or by those who attach themselves to Jesus in order to benefit from his suprahuman power and who, therefore, would distract him from his ministry of preaching the good news of the kingdom of God "to the other cities also." In each case, the ministry of Jesus is shown to be of a kind that will not be sidetracked by the intentions of human players in the drama (whether they be good intentions, as in 4:42, or bad intentions, as in 4:28–29). Instead, it is a ministry that is driven by the God whose plan is insuperable and unstoppable—a plan that bypasses Nazareth as the place of Jesus death.

At various points in Luke's Gospel, then, the audience hears of the divine necessity that Jesus' ministry is to be carried out across an extensive geographical area and is to climax in the giv-

Discovering Patterns

ing of his life in the city of Jerusalem. For the story to end in Nazareth contravenes the inevitable plan of God.

But there is even more to things than this. For as Luke's narrative shows, the Nazareth incident lays something of the foundations for Jesus' ministry, so that his sermon becomes unpacked in various ways throughout the following chapters of Luke's Gospel. For instance, whereas Jesus speaks of announcing "good news to the poor," that appellation applies not only to the economically poor (and Luke's Gospel makes clear that it applies certainly to them) but also to those with illness and physical disabilities, those who had entered into despised professions, those excluded from the normal definition of the "people of Israel's deity," those possessed by evil spirits, and any others that found themselves marginalized, the object of derision or simply in need (not least, needing forgiveness). They are among an expanded definition of "the poor."[25] The Isaianic program is outlined in the Nazareth incident as Jesus reads from Isaiah 61, but the fulfillment of that program finds its fulfillment in the narratives beyond that incident. For Jesus' death to have occurred in Nazareth would have prevented the Isaianic program from being fulfilled, obstructing the very plan of God. In the worldview of Luke, this is a theological impossibility.

Much the same pertains to the figures of Elijah and Elisha in relation to Jesus' ministry. Jesus himself recalls their importance when addressing his townspeople in the Nazareth incident. In fact, the people's rage surges after he speaks these words about Elijah and Elisha: "There were many widows in Israel in the time of Elijah, when the heaven was shut up three years and six months, and there was a severe famine over all the land; yet Elijah was sent to none of them except to a widow at Zarephath in Sidon. There were also many lepers in Israel in the time of the prophet Elisha, and none of them was cleansed except Naaman the Syrian."

---

25. See, for instance, Green, "Good News to Whom?"

These prophets were used by God to bring salvation to those beyond the boundaries of the people of Israel, and Jesus is implicitly styling his ministry on these two prophetic figures. Later episodes within Luke's Gospel seem designed to bring out precisely this typological relationship between Jesus and his prophetic forebears, Elisha and Elijah. Accordingly, just as Elisha had healed the Syrian general Naaman (2 Kgs 5:1–14) through the intercession of a young Jewish girl, so in Luke 7:1–10 Jesus heals the slave of a gentile centurion through the intercession of Jewish elders. Similarly, just as the prophet Elijah had raised to life the son of the widow Zarephath (1 Kgs 17:17–24), in Luke 7:11–15 (the very next episode to the Elisha-like episode of 7:1–10) Jesus raises from the dead the son of the widow of Nain.[26] While the contours of Jesus' public ministry are defined in the words Jesus' pronounces in the Nazareth incident, that ministry still requires enactment beyond the boundaries of the Nazareth incident itself. More must transpire beyond Nazareth if God's plan is to take effect, which it inevitably must, in the Lukan worldview.

Against these backdrops, the "rereader" of Luke's Gospel begins to see the futility of the efforts of the people of Nazareth in Luke 4, as they drag Jesus off to the side of the cliff; no matter how close they can get to carrying out their intentions, in the end their efforts run contrary to the will of God. Without knowing it, their designs against Jesus run contrary to the divine design for the outworking of Jesus' extended ministry.[27] Although the audience, and especially the "rereaders" of the Gospel, know that Jesus' death is necessary as part of the good news of God's saving initiative, they also know that at no point did the strategy

---

26. Compare especially the phrase "and he gave him to his mother" (καὶ ἔδωκεν αὐτὸν τῇ μητρὶ αὐτοῦ) in Luke 7:15 with the same phrase of 1 Kgs 17:23 (LXX: καὶ ἔδωκεν αὐτὸν τῇ μητρὶ αὐτοῦ). See further Evans, "Luke's Use of the Elijah/Elisha Narratives and the Ethics of Election."

27. Squires (*The Plan of God in Luke-Acts*, 173) finds there to be seven features of the inevitable divine plan that pertain to Jesus' ministry: "Jesus' preaching, travelling, betrayal, suffering, death, resurrection, return and judgement."

Discovering Patterns

of the Nazareth townspeople have any chance of success, precisely because it ran wholly against the grain of the unyielding plan of God for the unfolding ministry of Jesus.[28] Quite simply, it was not ordained for Jesus to die in Nazareth, since he had more to accomplish in his ministry and since his death had to occur elsewhere. In a Nazareth crisis that was swiftly leading to Jesus' death, divine initiative invaded the moment to ensure that the unstoppable plan of God would proceed and "make its way" to its inevitable goal. In accordance with the divine will, Jesus needed not simply to die any kind of death. Instead, he had to die *in Jerusalem* but *only after preaching the good news far and wide*, in fulfillment of an Isaianic program that resonated with the ministries of Elisha and Elijah. In this way, Jesus' death and his divinely-initiated resurrection are to be understood within the context of his words and deed that lie between the defining moments of Luke 4:16–30 and Luke 23–24.

This is precisely what Cyril of Alexandria tried to express in his commentary on Luke's Gospel, when he wrote: "He went through the midst of them without taking any notice, so to say, of their attempt; not refusing to suffer—for this reason he had even come—but as awaiting a suitable time. For it was now the commencement of his preaching, and it would have been unseasonable to have suffered before he had proclaimed the word of truth."[29]

If it is true that "for everything there is a season, and a time for every matter under heaven," a death for Jesus in Nazareth would have been "unseasonable" and untimely, and consequently, in Lukan terms of reference, would have been a theological impossibility.

---

28. So, for instance, Moessner, "Reading Luke's Gospel as Ancient Hellenistic Narrative," 138–39.

29. Cyril of Alexandria, "Sermon 12," *A Commentary upon the Gospel according to S. Luke*, 65.

COMPARING INCIDENTS OF DIVINE CAUSALITY

Having made reference above to the narrative of Acts, it is opportune to compare the episodes in Acts that have some resemblance to what has been proposed regarding the plotlines within Luke 4:30. Luke has no other episodes of "escape" within his Gospel, but enjoys recounting episodes of this kind in his narration in Acts—miraculous escapes from prison and/or from death. The point of recounting these episodes is not to claim that they all align themselves in precisely the same way with the plotline of Luke 4:28–30. The point is simply to demonstrate Luke's penchant for stories of supranatural involvement in what, to the "untrained" eye, would otherwise look like a curiously odd chain of cause-and-effect relationships.[30]

Peter's "escape" from prison offers one example, recounted particularly in Acts 12:6–11. There, we are told that, his chains falling off, Peter "went out" of the prison by means of angelic intervention. Here the angelic agency is noted for the benefit of the story's audience, but the narrative seems to imply that the characters in the story are unaware of the agency. Peter and the angel "pass by the first and second guard," evidently unnoticed. So too, the iron gates of the prison open automatically, again evidently unnoticed. For most of the human characters in the episode itself, Peter was there one minute, but not the next. Even Peter is said to have come to himself after the angelic rescue was completed. In this way, the episode compares well with the Lukan account of the Nazareth episode in 4:30, with Jesus simply departing from among those who held him in their grasp.[31]

The same is the case in Acts 5:17–24. There the high priest and all who were with him are said to be "filled with jealousy" over the apostles Peter and John, and consequently they have the two apostles arrested and put in prison. But things do not go according to the plan of the chief priests. Instead, "during the night

---

30. On the miraculous in Luke's Gospel and the Acts of the Apostles, see Talbert, *Reading Luke*, 241–46.

31. Further on this episode, see Strelan, *Strange Acts*, 263–73.

Discovering Patterns

an angel of the Lord opened the prison doors, [and] brought them [the apostles] out" (5:19). In his narration, Luke articulates the line of causality for this rescue explicitly in relation to "an angel of the Lord." But since the priests and the guards do not have recourse to this interpretation of the event, they are left in a quandary and without explanation as to what has happened. The irony of the Lukan account is hard to miss. So, in 5:21–24 we read how, in the morning, the high priest "sent to the prison to have them brought. But when the temple police went there, they did not find them in the prison; so they returned and reported, 'We found the prison securely locked and the guards standing at the doors, but when we opened them, we found no one inside.' Now when the captain of the temple and the chief priests heard these words, they were perplexed about them, wondering what might be going on."

Without recourse to a theology of the surprising initiative of God in relation to Jesus and his followers, the reader of the Lukan account would be as ill-suited to explain the events of that narrative as the chief priests and captain of the temple, for whom certain cause-and-effect relationships are simply illegible and inexplicable.[32]

Along with this we might compare the episode in Acts 16:25–26, where divine causality validates the legitimacy of the ministry of Paul and Silas. In prison, they pray and sing to God while all other prisoners listen. An earthquake shakes loose the doors and the chains of all the prisoners fall off. Too good to be true? Not if you're the author of Acts, whose view of cause-and-effect relationships includes space for the initiative of God. And so, in the episode of Paul and Silas, lines of causality are not explicitly stated, but neither do they need to be. The reader is simply to imagine the earthquake and its effects to be the product of divine initiative.[33]

---

32. Further on this episode, see ibid., 261–63.
33. Further on this episode, see ibid., 274–84.

Another episode in Acts shares with Luke 4:30 a notable "unexplained" dimension. In Acts 14, Paul is in Lystra and receives a mixed reception there. The end of his time in Lystra is recounted in Acts 14:19–20: "But Jews came there from Antioch and Iconium and won over the crowds. Then they stoned Paul and dragged him out of the city, supposing that he was dead. But when the disciples surrounded him, he got up and went into the city. The next day he went on with Barnabas to Derbe."

Whereas his persecutors found no life in Paul's body, whatever life there was in it became fully animated once again, almost immediately, so that he seems simply to hop up, walk about, and move on to the next city without any notable effects from the near-fatal stoning. It is even possible that Luke's auditors would have understood Paul to have been dead, as Rick Strelan forcefully proposes, and that this event is an episode of raising the dead, as in Acts 9:36–42 and Acts 20:7–12.[34] But whatever the historical basis of this event, the very oddity of Paul's recovery testifies to the primacy of theological narration in this instance. Consequently, readers are not to attribute Paul's remarkable recovery to some incredible physical vitality on his part, unlike Wangerin's depiction of the nimble Jesus. Instead, the reader is to imagine some special divine involvement in moving the scene from apparent death to inevitable advancement, not unlike the narrative of Luke 4:28–30 itself.[35]

---

34. Ibid., 243–51. Strelan argues as follows (ibid., 246–47): "The practice was that a person was stoned to death and the corpse then dragged around the streets and eventually out of the city. The point of the exercise was to denigrate the corpse. Even in death, the person was rejected by and ejected from the community of the living ... Paul had stones thrown at him, ... [then] his body was dragged through the streets and dumped outside of the city because the locals thought he was dead, and because they wanted to disgrace his body. The dead body of an unwanted outsider belonged outside the *polis*. It is this dragging of the body through and outside the town that suggests to me that Paul was dead. If the locals had simply thrown stones at him and knocked him out, they would not have performed this extra ritual."

35. Cf. Parsons (*Acts*, 202) writes: "This symbolic (or actual) death and resurrection bears witness again to the 'unhindered' nature of the gospel." For

Discovering Patterns

A further example of an event that has an unexplained causal dimension is found in Acts 28:1–6. While Paul was tending a fire on the island of Malta, a snake attached itself to Paul's hand. Shaking off the dangling creature, Paul is said to have "suffered no harm." From the perspective of human cause-and-effect relationships, the native people expected Paul "to swell up or drop dead." But because that does not happen, we are told that "they changed their minds and began to say that he was a god." Even if the Maltese people are shown not to have properly understood Paul's identity, they have nonetheless rightly recognized that human causality was not a factor in the situation. Instead, divine causality must be called upon to explain Paul's miraculous escape from death.[36]

Similar dynamics are evident, and explicitly so, in the Lukan account of Philip and the Ethiopian eunuch in Acts 8:26–40. That episode is marked out by a structural *inclusio* emphasizing suprahuman agency, with "the angel of the Lord" arranging the encounter between the two characters in 8:26 and "the Spirit of the Lord" transporting Philip away at the end of their encounter. And an oddity of the same magnitude as the events of Luke 4:30 is evident in Acts 8:39–40, where Philip is literally "there one minute and gone the next." So we read: "When they came up out of the water, the Spirit of the Lord snatched Philip away; the eunuch saw him no more, and went on his way rejoicing. But Philip found himself at Azotus." Here the Spirit of God transports a protagonist from one place to another, spanning perhaps twenty kilometers, with the protagonist simply "finding himself"

---

a discussion of narrations of Acts 14:19–20 in modern novels, see "Appendix 1" below.

36. Further on this episode, see Strelan, *Strange Acts*, 284–92. When recounted one after another, these rescue stories may give the impression that Luke's is a Gospel of personal triumphalism. But it is, of course, the plan of God that triumphs, not the prospects of particular individuals. The stoning of Stephen is a case in point. He experienced no divine rescue, but his death is nonetheless intertwined with the ongoing triumph of God in salvation history. For a study in the role of suffering in the theology of Luke, see Horton, *Death and Resurrection*.

in a new location. By comparison, the account in Luke 4:30 looks relatively simple and uncomplicated.[37]

Unlike Luke 4:30, some of these episodes from Acts explicitly specify that the "rescue" of the protagonist was carried out by suprahuman involvement. But in three instances in Acts, the agent of suprahuman involvement goes unmentioned—i.e., the restoration of Paul's health/life in Acts 14:19–20, the release of Paul and Silas in Acts 16:25–26, and the protecting of Paul from the effects of snake venom in Acts 28:1–6. But what all of the episodes have in common is their enunciation of Luke's conviction that, despite the recurrent hurdles that are placed before it, the emerging Jesus-movement strides on, animated by the Spirit of God. Precisely the same conviction is likely to explain the otherwise underdeveloped narrative of Luke 4:30, in which Jesus strides on, having just proclaimed the Spirit of the Lord to be upon him. If the events of Luke 4:30 are seen to be virtually "unbelievable," such an estimate is exactly in accordance with the spirit/Spirit of the Lukan narrative.

---

37. Further on this episode, see Strelan, *Strange Acts*, 85–89.

FIVE

Engaging the Audience

Subtlety as Strategy

IN SETTING OUT THIS proposal, one issue has been rumbling around that needs to be attended to directly: that is, the function of the narrative gap in relation to the "reading experience" of the audience. The proposal here is that the reader not only reads the text but that, in some sense, the text "reads" the reader.

THE ACT OF READING, AS THE TEXT READS THE READER

The conclusion of the Nazareth incident in Luke 4:28–30 may not simply function as an intriguing literary feature that provides a foothold into the Lukan theological worldview. It may, in fact, play a role in engaging the audience so as to challenge and/or reinforce the audience's interpretive options and predispositions, depending on the extent to which their interpretive predilections coincide with those of Luke's own worldview.

In this regard, it is important to note that Luke 4:28–30 does not simply arc *forward*—that is, to the end of the Lukan Gospel (i.e., to Jesus' death and resurrection) and beyond that into the Acts of the Apostles, where the typology of divine initiative transforming desperate situations is played out repeatedly. It also arcs *backwards* within the Lukan Gospel—in fact, to the very first episode of the Gospel. In Luke 1:5–56, Luke recounts the prehistory of the birth of John the Baptist, where divine initiative is everywhere, and is contrasted with human failure to expect and perceive divine initiative, as evidenced especially by John's father Zechariah. So, when he is told that Elizabeth's lifeless womb will be the place where a powerful instrument of God is to be birthed (i.e., John the Baptist), Zechariah's reply is a stupefied "How will I know that this is so? For I am an old man, and my wife is getting on in years" (1:18). His question is wholly understandable, of course, when the situation is analyzed in relation to human causality, since the body of his wife (and perhaps his own body too) is not a breeding ground from which life can emerge. But the theological substructures upon which the events of Luke 1 are recounted clearly demonstrate that Zechariah's worldview does not leave enough room for the surprising initiative of God in the realm of cause-and-effect relationships. The angel Gabriel says it distinctly: "nothing will be impossible with God" (Luke 1:37).

So when it comes to the Nazareth incident of Luke 4, the attempt to depict a cunning escape of one kind or another is to reduce the worldview of the narrative to the worldview adopted by Zechariah in Luke 1—a character whose worldview is shown to be deficient (or, perhaps, to have undergone a momentary lapse).[1] With the benefit of the stories of Luke 1, the audience might imagine that the storyline of Luke 4:30 is narrated oddly, but only if their terms of reference are theologically inadequate. The hearer of the Lukan Gospel is expected not to respond to Luke 4:30 in ways such as, "How did that happen? Maybe Jesus knew a secret tunnel." Nor: "Perhaps Jesus was a magical sorcerer." Nor: "Jesus must have had some sympathizers in the crowd." Nor: "Jesus must have blockaded the door and darted off on a horse." Regardless of whether the audience initially gives

---

1. Perhaps Mary may evidence a similar kind of "theological lapse" in 1:34, although that depends on the rhetorical force of her question "How can this be, since I am a virgin?" For instance, nowhere is Mary accused of failing to believe the angelic pronouncements in the way that Zechariah is (1:20), and nowhere is she penalized with an affliction, unlike Zechariah.

Engaging the Audience

consideration to lines of causality along lines such as these, the expectation seems to be that the audience will ultimately adopt an interpretation that the Lukan writings demonstrate to be the theologically preferred option—one involving divine involvement in some fashion.[2]

Whereas Luke 1 permits the audience to watch Zechariah fumble the issue of divine intervention in the events of history, Luke 4 puts the spotlight, in a sense, on the audience itself. If the narrative of that verse is found to be surprising and odd, then the informed rereader is expected to recognize that she has not yet aligned her worldview to coincide with that of the Lukan narratives, which presume and build on the conviction that the initiatives of God are often manifested in surprising and shocking ways. The rereader has to see the veracity of that conviction at the very start of Jesus' public ministry if she hopes to comprehend fully the significance of the story that transpires beyond the first public frames of Jesus' ministry.

In this way, then, Luke 4:30 serves purposes similar to a narrative parable—teasing the reader, taunting her to enter into its under-narrated folds and to find there the theological mystery that lies at the heart of the reality that the Lukan narrative testifies to: from hopeless situations, from daunting chains of human cause-and-effect relationships, God brings hopeful reality alive.

Instead of finding Luke 4:30 to be a narrative glitch that needs to be ironed out one way or another, it is best seen as a narrative taunt. It engages the audience, grabs their attention, asking questions of them regarding their own reading strategies (or "rereading strategies"), and forcing them to be expectant of further developments in this narrative that depicts the oft-times startling initiative of God in the historical realm.

---

2. John's Gospel demonstrates a similar narratological interest. In John 8:59, people pick up stones to throw at Jesus, but he hides and goes out of the temple. And in John 10:39, the people try to arrest Jesus, but he escapes from their hands.

Accordingly, Luke 4:30 lies right of the heart of the Lukan "eucatastrophe"—the sudden turn of events at the climax of a storyline, in which evil is turned aside and the good is established, even if only temporarily. Apparently first coined by J. R. R. Tolkien, the term "eucatastrophe" captures in itself the overthrowing of catastrophe by that which is good ("eu" being Greek for "good").[3] The Lukan Gospel is framed by two moments of prominent eucatastrophe, with the dead womb of Elizabeth (a personal eucatastrophe for Zechariah and Elizabeth) becoming the vehicle for life at the beginning of the Gospel, and the enwrapped corpse of Jesus becoming transformed in resurrection at the end of the Gospel. In-between the beginning and the end, there are a number of episodes that have a eucatastrophic dimension, being played out either in relation to personal stories of healings and exorcisms, or in relation to the national story of Israel, caught in the grip of foreign domination (Luke 3:1–2, 19–20) but now visited by the Messiah who will "guide our feet into the way of peace" (Luke 1:79).[4]

But the most dramatic of those intervening stories is the Lukan Nazareth incident. The drama of that episode's ending is notable and "eye-catching" precisely because the narrator chooses not to include mention of the suprahuman chain of causality that lies at the heart of the episode's outcome. Accordingly, since the outcome has no adequate explanation in relation to human causality, and since the narrator purposefully neglects to mention the necessary suprahuman involvement in the episode's outcome, the climax of the Nazareth incident grabs the audience's attention. Its bald narrativization helps to sharpen the focus of the eucatastrophe that the Lukan Gospel heralds. It is not really an occasion to fill a narrative gap through reflecting on potential human cause-and-effect relationships (as ingenious as those at-

---

3. Tolkien, "On Fairy-Stories," 60.

4. In the Lukan narrative, this eucatastrophe sets off a catastrophe in its wake: the rejection of the good news by a number of those within the covenant people of Israel.

tempts might be). Instead, by engaging the audience's curiosity, the narrative gap exposes the eucatastrophe of the Christian gospel in stark and glaring terms, thereby ensuring that Luke's preferred parameters for interpreting the story of Jesus are kept firmly and properly in place.[5]

Perhaps this is what Tolkien was referring to when he spoke of eucatastrophe as the unexpected twist in a story that transforms the virtual defeat of the protagonist into a moment of unexpected triumph, thereby offering "a piercing glimpse of joy . . . that for a moment passes outside the frame [of the story], rends indeed the very web of story, and lets a gleam come through."[6] In the eucatastrophic moment, "we see in a brief vision that the answer may be greater—it may be a far-off gleam or echo of *evangelium* [good news] in the real world."[7] According to Tolkien, eucatastrophe "produces its peculiar effect because it is a sudden

---

5. Tolkien's explication of eucatastrophe in "On Fairy-Stories" matches Luke's Gospel in two other regards, although it goes its own way in another. First, for Tolkien eucatastrophe is not achieved through the surprising introduction of a new character into the storyline who magically waves a wand and sorts it all out in a jiffy. Eucatastrophe, instead, emerges from within the parameters of the story of conflict and struggle that has already been established (see p. 64). Luke's Gospel depicts that involvement of the divine eucatastrophic initiator right from the start. Second, Tolkien notes that eucatastrophe "does not deny the existence of *dyscatastrophe*, of sorrow and failure: the possibility of these is necessary to the joy of deliverance; it denies (in the face of much evidence, if you will) universal final defeat" and consequently it participates in "*evangelium*, giving a fleeting glimpse of Joy, Joy beyond the walls of the world" (p. 62). Luke focuses on the catastrophic (or what Tolkien calls the "dyscatastrophic") in various episodes of Acts especially, not least the stoning of Stephen (Acts 7:54–60) and the murder of James the son of Zebedee (Acts 12:1–2). But third, when Tolkien depicts eucatastrophe in fairy stories as "a sudden and miraculous grace, never to be counted on to recur" (p. 62), his discussion may diverge somewhat from that of the canonical Gospel narratives. There, it might be more appropriate to say that eucatastrophe is "a sudden and miraculous grace that one can never discount from future happenings."

6. Tolkien, "On Fairy-Stories," 63. As Tolkien would later define it, eucatastrophe involves "the sudden happy turn in a story which pierces you with a joy that brings tears" (*The Letters of J. R. R. Tolkien*, 100).

7. Tolkien, "On Fairy-Stories," 62.

glimpse of Truth," a glimpse that suddenly puts everything into perspective: "your whole nature chained in material cause and effect . . . feels a sudden relief as if a major limb out of joint had suddenly snapped back."[8]

In this light, it needs to be noted that the turning points of the Jesus-novels considered in chapter 3 above do not qualify as "eucatastrophic" depictions, even if catastrophe is averted in those storylines through one means or another. In Lukan frames of reference, if the eucatastrophe of the gospel is truncated into a story about athleticism, or magical hypnotism, or the bonds of family or friendship, or heroic get-aways, then full-blooded eucatastrophe shifts into catastrophe, at least theologically speaking. This is the calamity that Luke's two volumes depict repeatedly in relation to the ethnic people of Israel. While some of them rejoice in the eucatastrophe that lies at the heart of the Jesus story, most seem ultimately to reject it, resulting (in Luke's point of view) in tragedy. Whether through the tragedy of rejection or through the simple recasting of the narrative in straightforward cause-and-effect relationships, in Lukan perspective whenever the eucatastrophic narrative is discarded, theological catastrophe takes its place.

COMPARING GAPS AND STRATEGIES

I have proposed that the gap of Luke 4:30 draws the audience into the narrative, in a sense, as an opportunity to challenge and/or refine the audience's skills of interpreting the "history" recounted in Luke's narratives. Notably, something similar has been proposed with regard to another considerable gap in Luke's storytelling. It is not only in Luke 4:30 where Luke seems almost to revel in placing a gap within his narrative, and where his audience is almost inevitably to conclude that there must be something significant that is not being recounted explicitly. The same seems to

---

8. Tolkien, *The Letters of J. R. R. Tolkien*, 100. On the same page he defines material cause-and-effect relationships as "the chain of death."

Engaging the Audience

be the case with the gap that appears at the conclusion of Acts 28—the very end of the Acts of the Apostles.[9]

Most of the second half of Acts (Acts 13–28) is dedicated to recounting Paul's contribution to the mission of the early Jesus-movement. In the later stages of that block of material, readers are led to expect that Paul will make an appearance before the emperor in Rome, where Paul's case will be heard, owing to the fact that he was a Roman citizen. This narrative arc is set in motion in Acts 25:11, when Paul declares, "I appeal to the emperor." The remaining four exciting chapters of the Acts narrative all transpire from this moment, with the prospect of a trial highlighted once again just prior to the close of Acts, with Paul recounting his story and pointing out that he "was compelled to appeal to the emperor" (28:19).

But the narrative of Acts stops short of reporting a trial episode. Instead, the expectations of the audience go unrealized and unfulfilled. The narrative closes with Paul preaching under house arrest with varying degrees of success, with the final words of Acts reading in this way (Acts 28:30–31): "He lived there two whole years at his own expense and welcomed all who came to him, proclaiming the kingdom of God and teaching about the Lord Jesus Christ with all boldness and without hindrance." No explanation is offered regarding what transpired for Paul within those two years; there is no mention of a court appearance before the emperor and no mention of what happened to Paul after those two years.

Various suggestions have been given as to why Acts leaves such a large gap at the point of its narrative ending. In the past, proposals have included speculation that perhaps the narrative had caught up with historical events; or perhaps Luke ran out of papyrus at that point; or perhaps Luke intended to write a third volume; or perhaps Paul simply lived the rest of his life in obscurity.

---

9. On the relationship of Luke's Gospel to the Acts of the Apostles, see footnote 14 in chapter 4 above.

More recently, however, it has become common to see the ending of the Acts narrative as serving an important literary and theological function. It needs to be noted, for instance, that the ending of Acts is not simply haphazardly constructed. Instead, it seems purposely to link back to the beginning of Acts through the theme of "the kingdom of God" that Jesus himself speaks of (compare Acts 1:3 and 28:23, 31); so too, it links back to the beginning of the Gospel of Luke through the theme of "the salvation of God" that is found in Luke's writings only in Luke 2:30, 3:6, and Acts 28:28.[10] The ending of Acts, then, appears to be intentionally constructed so as to reinforce its relationship to the beginning not only of the Acts narrative but of Luke's Gospel as well.

So Luke appears to have crafted his ending with a high degree of intentionality as to its literary relationship to other parts of his literary corpus. But this only makes it more notable that he has ended the narrative of Acts without supplying what he had so intently drawn the audience's attention to—the impending trial of Paul in Rome. To what purpose?

One of the most stimulating suggestions regarding this literary puzzle has been advanced by Daniel Marguerat. According to Marguerat, Luke orchestrates an expectation within the audience that he intentionally fails to satisfy in order to force a particular response within the audience, causing them to see things in a new light. For Marguerat, the ending of Acts engages the audience by means of its curious narrative gap, and challenges the audience to look at events through a particular angle of vision. When they set aside their expectations for how the narrative should be resolved (i.e., with Paul standing trial before the emperor) and instead see the curious ending from a fresh perspective, then the ending of Acts is recognized to be not curious at all, but in fact, wholly satisfying. But that literary satisfaction arises only when

---

10. On this, see Marguerat, *The First Christian Historian*, 207; Tiede, "Glory to Thy People Israel."

Engaging the Audience

the audience aligns its terms of reference along lines different to the ones they had come to expect. The key, for Marguerat, is the theme of trial. Luke develops the audience's expectation that they will witness Paul standing in the very courts of the emperor, on trial for his beliefs and practices. But although that trial is never recounted in the narrative, the trial theme itself is not displaced from the narrative. Instead, the audience is to see the closing of the Acts narrative as itself involving a trial, but a trial of another kind. In Luke's presentation, the trial theme begins to operate on two levels of meaning. On the first level, Paul is a prisoner whose trial is pending. It is on this level of things that the ending of Acts looks curious and seems unsatisfying. But the trial theme also becomes refracted onto another level of meaning in the final chapter of Acts. Although he is a prisoner, Paul is nonetheless shown to "summon" the local Jewish leaders to hear his gospel message (28:17), and in this way Luke's narrative puts them on trial before Paul's gospel. While some Jews believe that gospel message, Paul's final words in 28:26–27 suggest that the majority do not. In a trial in which the spotlight has moved from Paul as defendant to the Jewish leaders as defendants, those Jewish leaders have demonstrated their own culpability in the failure of the mission to the Jews, thereby relieving Paul himself of that liability. Having achieved that ironic twist in the trial theme, the narrative virtually ends, except simply to note Paul's continuing efforts to preach his gospel.

In this way, by predisposing his audience to expect a trial in Rome but by failing to narrate an actual legal proceeding against Paul himself, the audience is enticed to realign their expectations and to adopt a new understanding of things.[11] While their expectations of an impending trial are met, the trial itself is one of a wholly unexpected sort. The curious gap that Luke leaves in the narrative plotline if Acts 28 becomes, then, a moment in which the audience itself is challenged to "reread" and rethink

---

11. For a similar reading of the Johannine Gospel, see Lincoln, *Truth on Trial*.

situations along different lines. The audience is drawn into the story precisely because of the narrative oddity that is presented to them in the final chapter of Acts; having been drawn in, they are to find a resolution to the oddity in a fashion that is wholly consonant with contours of the narrative, even if that resolution is not articulated explicitly within the text.

Marguerat's proposal resonates well with an ancient view of what Luke was doing at the end of Acts. John Chrysostom, the fourth-century Christian theologian and exegete, had this to say about the seeming oddity of the ending of Acts (*Homily on Acts* 15):

> [Luke] brings his narrative to this point, and leaves the hearer thirsty so that he fills up the lack by himself through reflection. The pagans do the same; for, knowing everything [about a plotline] wills the spirit to sleep and enfeebles it. But he [Luke] does this, and does not tell what follows, deeming it superfluous for those who read the Scripture, and learn from it what it is appropriate to add to the account. In fact, you may consider that what follows is absolutely identical with what precedes.

We will return to this general point about "what is appropriate to add" in chapter 7 below. For now, it is enough to notice Chrysostom's view that Luke leaves the hearer "thirsty so that he [the reader] fills up the lack" in the plotline "through reflection." Much the same is proposed here with regard to Luke 4:30.[12] While that verse and the ending of Acts are not identical in their narrative strategies, they share certain features, permitting a correlation between what Luke seems to want his audience to do in Luke 4:30 and what he wants them to do at the end of Acts. In each case, the oddity of the narrative itself grabs the audience's attention and involves them in the interpretive loop by forcing them to ponder further about the function of the gap. In each

---

12. Puskas (*The Conclusion of Luke-Acts*, 91–96; see also p. 17) discusses the extent to which the final episode of Acts relates to Luke 4:16–30, with both episodes being characterized by an unusual ending.

case, the hearer is left "thirsty so that he fills up the lack" in the plotline "through reflection."

In chapter 7 below, consideration will be given to whether the oddity of Luke 4:30 may well operate in another way as well, grabbing the audience's attention in order to underline yet another dimension of the Gospel's inner-workings. But before that option is explored, we need to turn once again to the realm of the Jesus-novel, in order to consider those instances in which eucatastrophe has been graphically depicted by modern Jesus-novelists, as discussed in the following chapter.

6

Releasing the Captives

Eucatastrophe in Jesus-Novels

IN CHAPTER 3 ABOVE, the strategies for interpreting Luke 4:30 were noted in various Jesus-novels, none of which demonstrated any notion of full-blooded eucatastrophe. At this point, several other novels can now be overviewed that, to one degree or another, go some way towards maintaining the Lukan eucatastrophe. A survey of this kind brings to light the territory in which the eucatastrophic imagination might reside. The purposes of this chapter are, therefore, illustrative. A reader who prefers argumentation over illustration may advance to chapter 7 below, where yet another dimension of Lukan literary and theological artistry will be proposed, in the light of proposals advanced thus far.

EXAMPLES OF EUCATASTROPHIC NARRATION

One novel that does some justice to the eucatastrophe of the Lukan Nazareth episode is Robert Harrison's *Oriel's Diary*. The reason for this lies primarily in the narrative point of view adopted throughout the book. In Harrison's hands, the public ministry of Jesus is recounted from the viewpoint of a somewhat humorous angelic being, the high archangel Oriel (as the subtitle advertises: *An Archangel's Account of the Life of Jesus*). With that viewpoint established, the eucatastrophic moment can be

Releasing the Captives

narrated with ease. In this episode, unlike many others in the novel, the angelic world does not simply observe events in Jesus' ministry from above; instead, the angelic world involves itself in the eventual outcome of those events. And as a consequence, even if the literary merits of this example might be in question, in theological terms the example might well coincide with the eucatastrophic interests of the Lukan narrative.[1]

> The next thing I knew, they were half pushing, half carrying their former carpenter out of the synagogue and down the road to where the hillside has fallen away and there is a sheer drop into the valley below.
>
> There they held Jesus, just inches from certain death, while they argued about what to do next. There was a confusion of opinion . . . The commotion continued until one of the men shouted, "We can't do this to Joseph's son." To which someone replied, "But is he Joseph's son?" This stimulated a chant of "Bastard, bastard, bastard. Push him, push him, push him." I could see Archangel Michael growing more and more tense and hoped he wouldn't do anything stupid.
>
> Above the rising chants one of the women shouted, "Some people say he is the Son of God." This was the last straw. They took that to be blasphemy, and blasphemy, for Jews, is the ultimate crime, deserving immediate death. In the microsecond that followed, I simply prayed. Michael acted. He swooped down into the mob and blasted a path straight through the middle of them. While the people were standing, wondering why they had all stepped aside, Maff [i.e., Maphrael, Jesus' guardian angel] took the opportunity provided and guided Jesus to safety.
>
> The result was that the crowd stood dumbfounded as Jesus walked calmly through the middle of them and away from his home village.

Whatever one thinks of its levity, when judged by Lukan terms of reference this account has some theological merit, at

---

1. Harrison, *Oriel's Diary*, 50–51.

least in drawing lines of causality that stretch beyond what is perceptible to the naked eye.

But then Harrison might be in danger of undoing some of the eucatastrophic effect by appending a theologically problematic sentence to the end of the episode: "Jesus may be safe, but I expect that his Father will consider Michael's action to be undue interference." In Lukan perspective, eucatastrophic interference is never contrary to the will of God; for Luke, eucatastrophic initiative of any kind derives wholly from within the realm of God's will. Of course, the reader is probably expected to see the deficiency of Oriel's impression that Jesus' Father will be upset with the interference, since Harrison characterizes the angels as "hardworking spirits who serve their God loyally without always understanding what he is up to."[2] So the eucatastrophe is likely to be evident to the reader of Harrison's novel, even if it is misunderstood by the angelic characters of the storyline.

Along different lines, Michael Monhollon's *Divine Invasion* sets out an interpretation of the episode that is explicitly eucatastrophic, in which human observers themselves are given the key to unlocking the eucatastrophe (unlike Harrison's *Oriel's Diary*). For Monhollon (as with Harrison's novel), Jesus was rescued by an angel in Nazareth: "[A] burst of light, visible for only an instant, blinded them and sent members of the crowd stumbling into each other. Jesus, himself apparently unblinded, pushed his way through them and came down the hill." We will return to this interpretation again in the next chapter, since there is more to Monhollon's reading to consider, but because it requires substantial elaboration, it would detract us unnecessarily from our primary focus here. The main point to register here is simply that Monhollon offers a thoroughly eucatastrophic reading of the Lukan Nazareth incident.

In his book *Jesus of Nazareth* (1977), the conservative scholar William Barclay was set with the task of amplifying Anthony Burgess's script of Franco Zeffirelli's film *Jesus of Nazareth*,

2. Ibid., 5.

Releasing the Captives

changing "the script into narrative form."³ And in that narrative, the Nazareth incident is recounted in this way: "[T]hey began to hustle him to the cliff outside the town. When they came in sight of the cliff, however, the crowd seemed *somehow* less determined. Jesus offered no resistance whatever. He and the mob confronted each other. Quite suddenly and quite quietly, the crowd opened up in silence on either side to let him pass through, and Jesus walked serenely away."⁴

In this scripting of the episode, the narrator depicts a final confrontation between Jesus and the townspeople that is marked out by a lack of bedlam and disorder (notice the descriptors "no resistance," "quietly," "in silence," "serenely"). Is this a eucatastrophic recounting of the episode? Quite possibly, if the reader is to imagine that the lessening of the crowd's determination was accomplished by the moving of God's Spirit among them, like the Spirit hovering over the waters of chaos and bringing order in the creation account of Genesis 1. And the narration of the crowd opening up on either side of Jesus and letting him pass through the middle might call to mind the miraculous rescue of the Hebrews in Exodus 14. Perhaps eucatastrophe is alive and well here.⁵

Another example of a eucatastrophic fictional rendering of the Lukan Nazareth incident comes from Moelwyn Merchant's novel, *Jeshua*. The relevant section reads as follows:⁶

---

3. Barclay, *Jesus of Nazareth*, 7.
4. Ibid., 92, emphasis added.
5. Of course, much is being read into the simple word "somehow" in the phrase "the crowd seemed *somehow* less determined." Perhaps the outdoor air and the exercise of the walk helped to give them better insight into what they were doing. Or perhaps there is subtlety here, in that eucatastrophe can be seen by the eyes of faith even where it is invisible to the eyes of those who see but do not perceive. In this case, the single word "somehow" might not be indication of a non-omniscient narrator who is closing down the reader's imaginative curiosity; instead, it might be read to signal something akin to "let the reader understand" that something significant is going on here.
6. Merchant, *Jeshua*, 170.

[T]hey hurried him across the village to the brow of a steep hill. They were about to cast him over its brink when he turned to them. Without a word he withdrew from the clasping hands, ignored the clenched fists and the lifted boulders, raised his hand in blessing and passed among them, leaving no trace of his passage more than the keel of a ship in still waters. They remained in silence until they lost sight of him as he took the road towards the lake.

This attempt at fictionalizing the Nazareth incident comes close to the Lukan account in many ways. Even though it contains fictionalized elaboration, it is a clean and crisp account, much like Luke's own. It involves no standing-down of the crowd, unlike Barclay's account. Nazarene hands remain clasped, angered fists remain clenched, and dangerous boulders remain lifted in the air, while Jesus passes through their silenced midst. There are no acts of ingenious agility, no magic spells, no suddenly added characters, and no adjusted endings. The oddity of the Lukan staging remains intact, only to be enhanced. And as a consequence, the Merchant storyline seems to encapsulate nicely what the Lukan Gospel may be intent on capturing: the surreal strangeness that is often integral to divinely initiated eucatastrophe.

A FULL-BODIED EUCATASTROPHIC NARRATION

In contrast to the light touch exemplified by some authors of Jesus-novels, a fully amplified eucatastrophic narrativization is evident in the impressive novel *The Jerusalem Scrolls* by Brock and Brodie Thoene.[7] The final Jesus-story to be considered here, it is one worthy of ample attention because of the multi-faceted fashion in which the Thoenes develop a eucatastrophic reading in general accordance with some of the features that have already been noted in the chapters above.

The Thoenes' version of Luke 4 inserts their main character into the episode: i.e., Miryam, or Mary Magdalene, a renowned

---

7. Thoene, *The Jerusalem Scrolls*, 189–90.

and unapologetic economically secure woman who uses her sexuality as a tool for her own personal advancement (and ultimate deterioration). At the point in the narrative relevant to our interests, Miryam is infested with demonic inhabitants who torment her and craft her identity in a destructive fashion. In the episode recounting the Nazareth incident, other characters within the Thoene Jesus-novel include: Yeshua, who, of course, is Jesus; the "shammash," or the synagogue attendant; and Barak bar Halfi, a married man that Miryam has been totally devoted to since her youth, being unaware that he is actually a scoundrel. Both the shammash and Barak are orchestrators of the uprising against Jesus.

> Miryam . . . joined the chorus of accusers and shouted, "Stone him!" Miryam laughed, enjoying the show. The mob went wild! She was certain they were going to throw him off the precipice. And then it would be over. This great healer, this miraculous godly man, would not be able to save himself. Being righteous was no better than being wicked, Miryam thought. Either way people would find a way to despise you. And what they despised they would seek to destroy.
>
> It was impossible for Miryam to separate the howling of the crowd from the shrieking in her head.
>
> At the brink of the sheer drop, the crowd halted. On one side of Yeshua was the shammash, on the other, Barak bar Halfi.
>
> The shouting of the throng stopped, but not the screech of Miryam's inner voices.
>
> *Kill him! Push him over! He's no one! Arrogant! Full of pride! Who does he think he is? The Messiah?*
>
> Yeshua gazed into the eyes of the synagogue attendant.
>
> Yeshua knew the man. He knew them all. Those people who were determined to kill him . . . they had watched Yeshua grow up! And Yeshua knew them each well!

Even from a distance Miryam could see the shammash withdraw his hands from the teacher. In evident confusion he covered his eyes and stumbled backwards.

Then Barak [did the same] ... [W]ith Yeshua's steady examination of Barak's face, Barak released his hold as if he had been burned. His arms hung limply at his sides.

Yeshua stepped from between the two men. No one else moved forward to take him.

Suddenly all the attackers stepped back. No, fell back, cleaving a path through the mob.

For an instant more he searched every familiar face. His mother called his name in grief, but he did not acknowledge her voice.

The teacher strode from the brow of the hill into a stillness as complete as a tomb's.

Turning his back on Nazareth, he walked away from his hometown toward the north.

There are several features of this account that need to be appreciated. First, this scene helps to set up a narrative arc to the closing scenes of the Thoene's novel, where Jesus meets Miryam in the traditional (although flawed) interpretation that Mary/Miryam of Magdala was the woman of John 8:2–11 caught in adultery. By introducing Miryam into the Nazareth synagogue scene, the Thoenes have constructed an intriguing irony into their narrative. In the synagogue scene Miryam is shown to urge more strongly than anyone that Jesus be stoned, whereas in the later scene she herself is shown to be the potential victim of stoning because of her adulterous behavior. The roles are interlocked in the two scenes, with Miryam later finding herself in the place where Jesus had already been. But just as she had been part of the maddened Nazareth crowd that urged the stoning of Jesus, Jesus is the one who stands against the maddened crowd that urges the stoning of Miryam. And just as Jesus walks through the Nazareth crowd unharmed, so too the crowd around Miryam dissipates without acting on its venomous intent. The reader is left in no doubt of what has happened in the later incident, perhaps in parallel to the dynamics of the Nazareth incident: "Gentle mercy!

... [A]t that instant ... chaos had fallen from her. Dense confusion had parted."[8] As a result of her encounter with the one who had himself faced the prospect of being stoned, Miryam experiences mercy and hope, and her life is on the way to being reconstructed for good. The irony of Jesus' words of John 8 is even more poignant in relation to the narrative arc that the Thoenes have constructed, when the sinless Jesus of John says, "Let anyone among you who is without sin be the first to throw a stone at her"[9]—just as the people of Nazareth were intending to stone Jesus. In this way, the Nazareth incident plays a key role within the primary narrative arcs of the Thoene Jesus-novel.

Second, when all of its narrative parts are assembled, the Thoene's dramatization of the Nazareth incident qualifies as a case of eucatastrophe. Unlike the Jesus of some novels, the Thoene Jesus is fully and unapologetically divine, and it is from this divine nature that the eucatastrophe emerges.

To make the point about the divinity of Jesus in the Thoene novel, we can consider their two "Adonai" passages. The Thoenes occasionally enjoy the ironic technique of having a character pray to the creator God with words that apply specifically to Jesus. So, when the marriage feast at Cana has run out of wine, we are told that Jesus' mother Mary[10] "addressed her son 'Blessed art thou, Adonai, King of the universe, who creates for us the fruit of the vine and gives us wine to drink . . .'" At that point Miryam of Magdala is said to wonder in amazement "Had the woman really called her son *Adonai*," the reader knowing that she had.[11]

In case the reader has any doubt, the Thoenes use a similar technique late in the book to similar effect. Just prior to the scene in which Miryam is taken to Jesus as an adulteress needing to

8. Ibid., 261.
9. Replicated on ibid., 260.
10. Jesus' mother would have had the same first name as the Magdalene, but the Thoenes differentiate them to avoid confusion, calling Jesus' mother "Mary" and the Magdalene "Miryam."
11. Ibid., 33. The prayer is repeated word for word, compare ibid., 35, without a christological application, except by implication.

be stoned, singers in the temple sing out "Adonai, please save us! Adonai, please prosper us! Blessed is he who comes in the name of Adonai!" Then, after a period of silence in which only a cool wind moved through the temple, "Miryam gasped as Yeshua came forward . . . from the ranks of ordinary men."[12] Jesus in this episode may be coming in the name of Adonai rather than being Adonai, as in the Cana episode, but for the Thoenes there is very little difference to squabble about, as Jesus steps out "from the ranks of ordinary men" either way, in full relation to the creator Adonai. This is clear elsewhere in this same episode. Jesus promises living water to any who will trust in him, and Caiaphas the high priest is said to have "stumbled backwards and braced himself on the altar stones," with the mouths of the priests being "opened in astonishment and anger." Jesus "stood before Israel like a shepherd," and with the sun shining on him, "for an instant, Miryam thought his face seemed brighter than the rest."[13]

Notice how something similar happens in a further Thoene episode—precisely the episode that is the focus of this book, the Nazareth incident. At the outset of the Thoene's presentation of the Nazareth incident, a thirteen-year-old boy was called upon to read Psalm 80 to the Nazarenes assembled in the synagogue, as follows:

> Shepherd of Israel, listen!
> You who lead Yosef like a flock,
> you whose throne is on the cherubim, shine out!
> Before Ephraim, Benjamin, and Manasseh, rouse your power;
> And come to save us.
> God, restore us!
> Make your face shine, and we will be saved.[14]

As we have seen, the Thoene novel will later depict Jesus standing "before Israel like a shepherd" with his face seeming to shine "brighter than the rest." But here, in the Nazareth incident,

12. Ibid., 252.
13. Ibid., 252–53.
14. Ibid., 187.

the Thoenes continue the episode by recounting how Jesus was visibly moved by this acclamation about the "Shepherd of Israel" who is called upon to rouse his power and restore Israel by making his "face shine" so that Israel "will be saved." So the Thoene narrative continues: "The words [of Ps 80] roused Yeshua. He lifted his chin and smiled at the boy. The rebbe's face [i.e., Jesus' face] shone with pleasure," in which case we see a proleptic fulfillment of the words of Psalm 80 within the Nazareth episode. Consequently, Jesus goes to the front of the synagogue to read from Isaiah that "The Spirit of Adonai is upon me."[15] But lest the reader should miss the point, the Thoene's reinforce Jesus' identity by narrating the theme of the face of God "shining out." The dramatic irony arises for those with eyes to see, as the theme of the "shining face of God" links the scripture reading in the Nazareth synagogue (i.e., Ps 80) to the very events that were unfolding before their eyes of the people of Nazareth.[16] No wonder Jesus can speak of scripture being fulfilled "today," as his face shines out as an embodiment of the shining face of God.

These are examples of the sort of thing that happens repeatedly in the Thoene narrative. So when Jesus in Nazareth faces down the opposition among the ranks of his fellow townspeople later in the Nazareth incident, this has nothing to do with some incredible quality that lay innate within Jesus' fully-human character, for instance, as in the Graves novel. It is instead to be attributed wholly to divine causality.

In this way, the Thoene dramatization of the Nazareth eucatastrophe taps directly into the extremely high theology that animates their "Adonai" episodes. Other features of their depiction of the Nazareth incident also play into this theological portrait of Jesus. For instance, the Thoenes put emphasis on the fact that Jesus was "knowing them [the people of Nazareth]

---

15. The theological depth that the Thoenes give to the Nazareth incident is further enhanced by having the account of the "sacrifice of Isaac" in Gen 22 as the first scriptural reading of the day.

16. Note the similarity of this to the proposal of chapter 7 below.

all well"—a double-entendre worthy of the canonical evangelist John. At one and the same time Jesus' knowledge of his townspeople points simply to his acquaintance with his own neighbors and, more profoundly, to his full understanding of them, since the creator knows his creatures absolutely.

Moreover, in the Nazareth incident those intent on oppressing Jesus are shown to fall away from him when he looks at them: "Suddenly all the attackers stepped back. No, fell back." Is it a coincidence that the same two verbs, "to step back" and "to fall," denote the action of John 18:6 (ἀπέρχομαι and πίπτω), in which those who have come to take Jesus away step back and fall to the ground when Jesus utters the double-entendre *ego eimi* ("I am he," meaning "I am Jesus of Nazareth," but also referencing the Divine Name)? Subtle intertextual tropes like this are standard fare in the Thoene's work. If such a trope is intended here, it would be another indication of the Thoene's dramatization of the Lukan Nazareth incident in relation to the divine power of one who is worthy to utter the divine *ego eimi*.

This raises a third aspect of the Thoene depiction of the Nazareth incident that correlates to features discussed in earlier chapters of this book. If the verbs "step back" and "fall" are subtle gestures to the Johannine arrest scene (where, like the Lukan Nazareth incident, Jesus is led away in the clutches of those with ill-intent), the Thoenes are following the likely lead of Luke and enhancing the link between the Nazareth incident and the passion/resurrection narratives. That this is an intentional link on their part is suggested by two other subtleties of the Thoene narrative. First, in the Thoene's Nazareth episode Jesus is teased by people with taunts that recur again when he later will hang from the cross. So in the Thoene Nazareth incident, some of Jesus' townspeople say: "This great healer, this miraculous godly man, would not be able to save himself." The irony is great, of course, since the reader is to know that, at least when it comes to the crucifixion, Jesus could indeed "save himself" (or perhaps call upon angels to have himself saved), but he chooses not to (as in the Synoptic account of his arrest in the Gethsemane garden). But just as the Nazareth townspeople taunt him, so too do the "leaders" attending his crucifixion, who say "He saved others; let him save himself!" (Luke 23:35). So too the soldiers mock him: "If you are the King of the Jews, save yourself!" (Luke 23:37). The theme of Jesus saving himself from his oppressors links the Thoenes' version of the Nazareth incident to the canonical crucifixion scenes.

A second indication that the Thoenes expect the Nazareth incident to be read in relation to the crucifixion and resurrection of Jesus might be indicated by their mention of Jesus walking away from the "brow of the hill" in Nazareth into "a stillness like that of a tomb." This is a way of signaling a movement from a deadly hill to a still tomb, a movement that will be replicated for Jesus again in Jerusalem, in parallel to the Nazareth incident. In this dramatization, Jesus' "release" at Nazareth is not a prefigurement of his later resurrection, as we might expect, but of his move from hillside cross to tomb. But regardless of how the linkage is configured, the Thoenes seem intent on making that link nonetheless.

In all of these ways, the Thoene account seems to score the highest points for its narrative complexity and theological attentiveness. It does the most justice to and enhances the Lukan theology of eucatastrophe that undergirds the Nazareth incident itself and lashes it to the accounts of Jesus' crucifixion and resurrection.

◆ ◆ ◆

Having observed examples of eucatastrophic narration of Luke 4:30 in a variety of Jesus-novels, one further possibility needs to be considered regarding the interpretive potential of the gap in Luke 4:30—a possibility given consideration in the following chapter.

SEVEN

Constructing Arcs

The Christological Fulfillment of Psalm 91

THE PREVIOUS CHAPTERS HAVE offered a simple reading of Luke 4:30. In this chapter, I want to "push the boat out" just a bit further, building on the proposals of earlier chapters while entertaining a further interpretive option that would seem to fall within the orbit of Luke's literary expertise—not least, his evident delight in constructing literary subtleties within his narrative.

In order to frame this final interpretive possibility, attention will initially be given to the scene of Jesus' temptation in Luke 4:1–13—an episode separated from Luke's recounting of the Nazareth incident in Luke 4:16–20 by only two verses that overview the early growth of Jesus' reputation (Luke 4:14–15). In Luke's presentation, the Nazareth incident is a defining moment for Jesus, a moment when he began to articulate the significance of his ministry in terms of its scriptural configuration. Notably, then, the temptation episode and the Nazareth episode are consistent in their depiction of Jesus. In both episodes, Jesus engages in conflict (with Satan and with the townspeople, respectively), and in each Jesus is shown to recite Scripture when defining his own perception of his ministry. Jesus' replies to Satan's three temptations, for instance, involve the recitation of Scripture on each occasion (Luke 4:4, 8, 12). The same Jesus who recites Scripture to Satan is the Jesus who reads with intent from Scripture in the

Nazareth episode (i.e., Jesus "unrolled the scroll and found the place where it was written . . ." 4:17).[1] Accordingly, the very first words that we hear from Jesus' mouth in Luke's Gospel are the words of Scripture, in both the temptation narrative and the Nazareth incident.

If Jesus says nothing other than the words of Scripture in the temptation scene and the opening of the Nazareth incident, Satan himself also finds the opportunity to cite Scripture in the temptation episode. As if he has learned from the first two temptations that Jesus cherishes the words of Scripture, in his third temptation of Jesus Satan recites Scripture as part of that temptation. Those scriptural words that Satan cites need now to be given full consideration, in relation to the proposals set out in the preceding six chapters of this book.

SCRIPTURE, CHRISTOLOGY, AND FULFILLMENT

According to Antonio in Shakespeare's *The Merchant of Venice*, "the Devil can cite Scripture for his purpose."[2] The temptation narratives in the Gospels of Matthew and Luke provide the biblical foothold for this claim, with their depiction of Satan citing Scripture to suit his own interests (Matt 4:5-7; Luke 4:9-12). There, Satan recalls a passage from Scripture in his efforts to "test" Jesus and, ultimately, to distract him from the course that the Gospels proceed to narrate in their accounts of Jesus' public ministry.

The scriptural passage that Satan cites in the temptation scene of Luke 4 is Ps 91:11-12. The Satanic "test" is recounted in this way in Luke's Gospel (4:9-11):

> If you are the Son of God, throw yourself down from
> here, for it is written, "He will command his angels con-

---

1. The motif of Jesus recounting Scripture carries on in Luke 4:25-27, in which he recalls episodes pertaining to Elijah (1 Kgs 17:1; 18:1-2) and Elisha (1 Kgs 17:8-9; 5:14), as discussed in the sub-section "Proposing a Different Christological Arc" in chapter 4 above.

2. Shakespeare, *The Merchant of Venice*, Act 1, Scene 3.

cerning you, to protect you," and "On their hands they will bear you up, so that you will not dash your foot against a stone."

In his reply, Jesus rebuffs the Satanic temptation with other words from Scripture: "Do not put the Lord your God to the test" (4:12, citing Deut 6:16). If each character has deployed a textual missile in a contest of scriptural interpretation, the Lukan narrative depicts Jesus as the victor in the contest.

But if the Satanic voice has been silenced, it remains to be considered whether the scriptural passage that Satan introduced remains in play within the Lukan narrative, and if so, in what fashion? Is the reader to think that a christological interpretation of Ps 91:11-12 is itself misguided? Or, accepting a christological reading of Ps 91:11-12, is the reader to think only that Satan's application of that passage to the temple testing is misguided?

In what follows, it will be suggested that a christological interpretation of Ps 91:11-12 lies embedded within the Lukan narrative, although in a fashion that runs contrary to the fulfillment motif proposed by Satan in the Lukan temptation account. Psalm 91 is indeed a christological Psalm (as Satan rightly assumed), but its fulfillment has nothing to do with Satan's own attempt to force its fulfillment before its time.

It is instructive to note that the earliest interpretations of Psalm 91 in proto-orthodox writings of the second through fourth centuries CE presume a christological interpretation of the Psalm to be legitimate (so Irenaeus, Tertullian, pseudo-Ignatius, and Augustine).[3] This view seems to fall in line with

---

3. So Irenaeus, *Against Heresies*, 3.23.7; Tertullian, *Against Marcion* 4.24 (cf. *Against Praxeas* 1); Augustine, *On the Psalms* 91.16. The so-called *Letter to the Philippians*, credited to Ignatius but more likely to have been pseudonymously written in the middle of the third century CE, seems to confirm this christological reading of Ps 91:11-12. The point is not wholly clear from the author's initial charge that, when quoting from Ps 91:11-12, Satan had the audacity "to read in Scripture concerning Him" (§10). Nonetheless, that a christological reading of those verses is not in dispute is confirmed by the author's next sentence. There he goes on to cite Ps 91:13 christologically, dem-

Constructing Arcs

the temptation narrative of Matthew's Gospel, and probably of Mark's Gospel as well. Mark's Gospel includes a very brief version of the temptation: "And he was in the wilderness for forty days, being tested by Satan, and he was with the wild animals, and the angels were serving him" (1:13). It is sometimes noted that the influence of "Psalm 91:11 may . . . hover in the background" of the phrase "the angels were serving him,"[4] or that Mark 1:12–13 "has apparently been influenced by Ps. 91.11, 13."[5] More explicit in this regard, however, is Matthew's Gospel. The Matthean account of the temptation narrative concludes with the mention of angels coming to Jesus and waiting on him (Matt 4:11). With the motif of angelic protection having been introduced into the Matthean temptation narrative through Satan's quotation of Psalm 91 (Matt 4:6), that motif seems then to find its christological fulfillment even within the temptation narrative itself, at its termination point, when angelic visitors come to serve him.

The Lukan Gospel, however, makes no mention of angelic visitation at the end of its temptation account. Instead, the Lukan text simply notes that the devil "ended every temptation" and "departed from him [Jesus] until an opportune time" (4:13). Consequently, if a subtle gesture to the christological fulfillment of Ps 91:11–12 is evident in one or two of its canonical siblings, Luke's Gospel offers no suggestion that the Psalm finds christological fulfillment at the end of the temptation narrative. Without

---

onstrating that Satan's audacity was not in reading Ps 91:11–12 christologically but in failing to continue his recital of the Psalm. As the author points out, the very next verse of the Psalm (Ps 91:13) prophesies (when read christologically) that Jesus himself will defeat Satan and his minions ("You will tread on the lion and the adder, the young lion and the serpent you will trample under foot").

4. Boring, *Mark*, 48.

5. Watson, *A Guide to the New Testament*, 159. The christological interpretation of Psalm 91 corresponds well with Adamic interpretations of Jesus (which many find allusions to in Mark's brief reference to Jesus being among the wild animals), since Ps 91:13 itself includes Adamic dimensions (with the mention of the adder or serpent being trodden on under foot, in reversal of the serpent striking the heal of Adamic humanity, Gen 3:15). See also footnote 13 below.

mention of an angelic visitation at the close of the temptation story, Luke's Gospel fails to supply a gesture towards the christological fulfillment of Psalm 91 within that account.[6]

SEARCHING FOR A CHRISTOLOGICAL ARC OF FULFILLMENT

This curiosity regarding the apparent non-fulfillment of Psalm 91 within the Lukan narrative seems to have captured the attention of some early Christian interpreters. The inclusion of Ps 91:11–12 within the temptation narrative raises expectations that the scriptural passage would ultimately find its christological fulfillment within the narrative—not least since so many other passages from the Psalm are shown to have christological fulfillment within Luke's Gospel (see the subsection, "Supporting the Proposed Christological Arc," below). Without the scriptural prophecy of Ps 91:11–12 finding its fulfillment in the temptation account (as in Matthew, and probably in Mark), Luke's narrative sets up the prospect that the christological prophecy might well be fulfilled in some event after the temptation narrative. The assumption of some early Christian interpreters seems to have been that one needs only to remain attentive to the prospect of finding how the narrative arc is fulfilled in order to find it.

Where did early interpreters of Luke's Gospel find the arc of prophecy (begun in Luke 4:10–11) to reach its christological

---

6. The point gains in interest the more we imagine Mark's Gospel to have circulated widely prior to the composition of Luke's Gospel. (See, for instance, Bauckham, *Gospels for All Christians*.) For if Mark's Gospel shows some interest in making a gesture towards the christological fulfillment of Psalm 91 even within the temptation scene itself (as noted above), it is all the more striking that Luke does not share in this interest, despite the precedent for it and, perhaps, the (presumably) widespread assumption that this is how Psalm 91 is to be understood as christologically fulfilled. Moreover, instead of postulating a source used independently by Luke and Matthew, if we imagine that Luke made use of Matthew (as defended by Goodacre, *The Case against Q*), the christological fulfillment of Psalm 91 within the temptation scene itself would have been all the more entrenched as a trope in the reading repertoire of early Jesus-followers.

fulfillment? Clearly, Ps 91:11-12 cannot be read in relation to the account of Jesus' crucifixion. Since Jesus did not experience an angelic rescue when hanging on the cross outside the walls of Jerusalem, interpreters looked elsewhere in their interests of closing up the arc from scriptural prophecy (introduced at 4:10-11) to narrative fulfillment of that prophecy.

Augustine, the theological giant from the late fourth century and early fifth century, looked to the ascension narrative as the point of closure for the arc of prophecy-fulfillment that is set in motion in Luke 4:10-11. Envisioning angelic service to be involved in the ascension of Acts 1:9-11, Augustine writes: "We need not therefore wonder that our Lord was raised up to heaven by the hands of Angels, that His foot might not dash against a stone" (*On the Psalms*, 91.16).[7]

There is arguably a narrative foothold for this interpretation since, immediately after Jesus ascends into the heavens, two angelic figures explain his ascension to the disciples (Acts 1:10-11). And Luke's use of passive verbs to refer to Jesus' ascension (e.g., "he was lifted up")[8] might be thought to permit the notion of angelic agency (although Luke explicitly says in Acts 1:9 that "a cloud took him out of their sight").

On the other hand, the description of angelic involvement outlined in Ps 91:11-12 does not match the ascension narrative very well. This is evident in the fact that, when linking Psalm 91 to the Lukan ascension motif, Augustine is required to underplay any sense of angelic *deliverance* from Ps 91:11 (i.e., "to protect you," διαφυλάσσω in the LXX and Luke 4:10).[9] Augustine virtually admits this to be a problem when he notes that "Christ was raised up in the hands of Angels, when He was taken up into heaven: not that, if Angels had not sustained Him, He would have

---

7. Nicene and Post-Nicene Fathers[1] 8:451.
8. ἀνεφέρετο, Luke 24:51; ἐπήρθη, Acts 1:9; ὁ ἀναλημφθείς, Acts 1:11.
9. According to Louw and Nida (*Greek-English Lexicon of the New Testament*), διαφυλάσσω suggests "to guard or protect something in order to keep it safe or free from harm."

fallen: but because they were attending on their King." By sitting lightly to the narrative details that are most explicit in Ps 91:11 (i.e., the motif of angelic deliverance and protection), Augustine can link a christological interpretation of that Psalm to the ascension account. Knowing that the match is slightly awkward, he explains the mismatch away by underplaying the motif of angelic protection that is featured explicitly in Ps 91:11.

Another ancient interpretive strategy presents itself as well, one that follows different contours even if it is driven by the same interest in arcing the fulfillment motif to a later point in the story of Jesus. In Luke 22:43-44, the audience observes an angelic visitation at the time of Jesus' "last temptation" in the Garden of Gethsemane (or as Luke puts it in 22:39, "the Mount of Olives"). While praying that the cup be removed from him, Jesus nonetheless expresses his wish that the will of God should ultimately transpire. At that point in the narrative, the passage reads: "Then an angel from heaven appeared to him and gave him strength. In his struggle [ἐν ἀγωνίᾳ] he prayed more earnestly, and his sweat became like great drops of blood falling down on the ground" (22:43-44).

These verses have often been thought to represent a scribal insertion into the Lukan text. The instability of these verses within the extant texts of Luke's Gospel has suggested to most analysts of the textual tradition that Luke 22:43-44 arose at some point in the second century.[10] If this is correct, it seems as though

---

10. The reasons for thinking that these verses are a later insertion have tended to be three: (1) these verses are not found in some of the earliest manuscripts of Luke's Gospel, manuscripts from diverse geographical regions; (2) some manuscript families insert them after Matt 26:39, suggesting their instability within the textual tradition; (3) some manuscripts designate them as distinct from Luke's Gospel through the use of special symbols that normally indicate that a passage is spurious, corrupt or doubtful in some way. For reasons of this kind, the editors of the standard Greek edition of the New Testament (NA27/ USB4) give the omission of these verses an "A" reading (on a scale of A through D, with A being the most secure interpretation of the data), indicating that there is little doubt in their minds that the verses represent a later insertion. See Omanson, *A Textual Guide to the Greek New Testament*, 150; Ehrman, *Misquoting Jesus*, 139-44.

Constructing Arcs

a scribe saw this portrait of Jesus' suffering in prayer to be helpful in countering the rising "heresy" often called "Docetism" (a form of Gnosticism). The Docetic instinct was to eradicate the humanity of "the Word made flesh," usually on the supposition that the material world is an obstacle to salvation, having been created by a lesser or an evil god. On these premises, the divine Word of God who entered this world simply could not have been intricately enfleshed within a human body and did not envelope a human identity in any fashion. Against the backdrop of this rising heresy, a well-intentioned scribe seems to have seen fit to insert a portrait that strongly countered Docetic interests by emphasizing Jesus' turmoil and suffering—that is, his humanity.

Accepting this interpretation of the origins of Luke 22:43–44, however, may not fully explain the content of those verses.[11] An interest in undermining Docetic interpretations does not necessarily require motifs of angelic visitation and strengthening. The insertion of only the second sentence (i.e., Luke 22:44) would have been enough to satisfy the scribe's anti-Docetic interests. Does this mean, then, that the insertion theory is implausible, and that we should cast our lot with the minority of scholars who have challenged the theory of scribal insertion in this case?[12]

---

11. This is rightly pointed out by Clivaz, "The Angel and the Sweat Like 'Drops of Blood,'" 439: "the anti-docetic argument could explain the interpolation of Jesus' agony and sweat in Luke 22:44 pretty well, but it does not explain why Luke 22:43's description of the angel should also have been added." But, as I hope to show, an anti-docetic interest in (the interpolation of) Luke 22:44 coincides with interest in the fulfillment of Psalm 91 in Luke 22:43 (similarly interpolated). What better way to illustrate the humanity of Jesus than to depict him requiring angelic assistance?

12. See, for instance, Brown, *The Death of the Messiah*, vol. 1, 180–85; Clivaz, *L'Ange et la sueur de sang*, 455–608; Clivaz, "The Angel and the Sweat Like 'Drops of Blood.'" One of Brown's arguments pertains precisely to the argument of this chapter (*Death of the Messiah*, 184): "would a copyist not have hesitated about adding a passage that apparently made an angel superior to Jesus, strengthening him?" The point is moot if the motivation for the proposed inclusion is to confirm the scriptural fulfillment of Psalm 91—itself a Psalm read christologically (and "Adamically") by Jesus-followers in the early centuries of the Common Era.

I need to be clear that the argument of this chapter is not affected by whether Luke 22:43–44 is a scribal insertion or not. In my view, it is more likely that Luke 22:43–44 is, in fact, a scribal insertion, and I will articulate my larger case in relation to this probability. But in Appendix 2 below, I will also signal how my larger case would operate should it be the case that Luke 22:43–44 is, in fact, original to the Lukan Gospel, even though that is not the way I see things. And so, in the following paragraphs, I will articulate the larger case on the basis that Luke 22:43–44 is not original to the Lukan Gospel but is a scribal insertion, motivated not simply by an anti-Docetic interest—since that interest alone cannot explain everything (as detractors of the "insertion" theory rightly point out). It is only when a christological understanding of Ps 91:11–12 is brought into the frame that the motivation behind the scribal insertion is fully explained.

The verses known to us as Luke 22:43–44 represent more than a mere focusing upon Jesus' humanity for anti-Docetic effect; as we have seen, such a view has little explanatory force in relation to the presence of the angel in these verses. Taking that aspect into account, Luke 22:43–44 represents a very early attempt by a discerning scribal interpreter to fix up what he perceived as a narrative deficiency in Luke's Gospel. The scribe has noticed that, because Luke's Gospel does not conclude the temptation account with a reference to an angelic visitation, Ps 91:11–12 has no christological fulfillment within that Lukan episode (unlike Matthew's Gospel explicitly, and probably Mark's Gospel implicitly). Knowing that Ps 91:11–12 needs christological fulfillment within the Lukan narrative, the perceptive scribe added to the Gethsemane drama, supplying an explicit grounding point for the prophecy-fulfillment motif, and doing so in a manner that permitted him to deprecate Docetic convictions at the same time. The result is an angelic visitation to an incontrovertibly human Jesus in order to assist that very human figure in his time of struggle. The angel of this scribal insertion "protects" Jesus (it might be said) by causing him to regain his strength in a

Constructing Arcs

time of excruciating anguish ("sweat like great drops of blood"), when the temptation to avoid the cross is as real and poignant as ever. In that context, the angel simply strengthens this recognizably human (but not merely human) Jesus, "bearing him up" (in a sense) in order that he might carry on in his God-ordained course.

In this reconstruction, not only is an anti-Docetic interest in play in the scribal insertion of Luke 22:43–44, so too is an interest in securing the christological fulfillment of Psalm 91 within Luke's Gospel. The two interests have gone hand in hand. Arguably, in contrast to Augustine's underplaying of the motif of angelic protection, the unknown scribe may have done better justice to the Psalm's emphasis on angelic protection, even if the semantic meaning has shifted somewhat from "protecting" to "strengthening"—or better, perhaps, to "protection through strengthening."

Further to his credit, the scribe's decision to link the christological prophecy of Psalm 91 to the Lukan Gethsemane story by way of a two-sentence insertion probably resulted from the fact that the conclusion of the Lukan temptation account speaks of Satan wanting to return (i.e., to tempt Jesus) at an "opportune" time. Probably in the scribe's view, it was the Gethsemane scene that qualifies as a good candidate for that Satanic return.[13] This

---

13. The parallel between the third temptation on the Temple and the Garden of Gethsemane has been noted by commentators. See, for instance, Meynet, *L'Évangile de Luc*, 180, 183. There may be no stronger candidate within Luke's Gospel for the Satanic return to Jesus than the Garden of Gethsemane. Luke's mention of Satan entering into Judas in Luke 22:3 puts Satan in the arena of events leading up to Jesus' death, but does not itself qualify as a temptation of Jesus; it is merely a Satanic orchestration of events that put Jesus into a position to be tempted. Note that Mel Gibson's film *The Passion of the Christ* puts Satan's "opportune time" in the Gethsemane Garden, where he tempts Jesus with words like "Do you really believe that one man can bear the full burden of sin?" It is also in that scene that Jesus crushes the head of a serpent that had been sent from beneath Satan's garments—itself a fulfillment of Ps 91:13, against the backdrop of Gen 3:15. Something similar is evident in Wangerin's *Jesus*, in which Satan appears as Jesus hangs on the cross (the "opportune time"), and there tempts him with coming down from the cross with words

is likely to explain his terminological choice in 22:44, when using the Greek word ἀγωνία. While this word may well depict psychological "anguish," "anxiety," or "agony," it can also convey the sense of a "contest" or a "struggle" with an opponent.[14] Incorporating a sense of struggle into the Gethsemane account follows on from Luke 4:13, with its foreshadowing gesture (i.e., "until an opportune time") taunting the reader to discover its narratological fulfillment. For the well-intentioned scribe, the contest between Jesus and Satan that was first displayed in the temptation scene is now being played out again in the Garden of Gethsemane, with the agonistic Satan testing Jesus' fidelity one final "opportune time."[15]

We have seen reason to think, then, that the scribal insertion of Luke 22:43-44 represents an ingenious attempt to close up the narratological arc regarding the christological fulfillment of Ps 91:11-12 as part of an interest to fend off a Docetic perception of Christology and salvation history. The passage is ingenious in accomplishing that goal both briefly and lucidly. But despite the astuteness of the mind that these verses derive from, that mind is most likely not Luke's.

PROPOSING A DIFFERENT CHRISTOLOGICAL ARC

If Ps 91:11-12 is not fulfilled christologically in the way that Augustine and an unknown scribe imagined, is it the case that Luke missed an opportunity to narrate the christological fulfill-

---

echoing the temptation narrative of Luke 4 and, in particular, Ps 91:11-12 (ibid., 318): "If you are the Son of God . . . fear nothing. Prove everything. Pitch your body headlong down. His angels out to catch you and bear you up."

14. ἀγωνία is commonly synonymous with ἀγών; see Thayer, *A Greek-English Lexicon of the New Testament*, 10, where the first entry for ἀγωνία appears as "equivalent to *agôn*." See also "ἀγωνία," in Liddell et al., *A Greek-English Lexicon*, 19, where its primary definition is a "contest" or "struggle for victory." See now especially Clivaz, *L'Ange et la sueur de sang*, 347-454.

15. As Moberly writes (*From Eden to Golgotha*, 93n14): "The point is the intensity of Jesus' wrestling in prayer (presumably to defeat Satan and the powers of evil) rather than any mental anguish as such."

ment of Ps 91:11-12 within his Gospel? Of course that must always remain a possibility. But instead of jettisoning the search for a completed narrative arc within Luke's Gospel, one other possibility presents itself: that is, finding the christological fulfillment of Ps 91:11-12 in the next main episode of the Lukan Gospel—namely, the Nazareth incident of Luke 4:16-30.[16]

We have already noted how the ending of the Lukan Nazareth episode exposes a narratological gap that tantalizingly draws its readers into an interpretive matrix that energizes a particular worldview regarding divine causality. Perhaps it is within that same tantalizing gap that the christological fulfillment of Ps 91:11-12 is to be found within Luke's Gospel. In this prospect, while Matthew closes up the arc of narratological fulfillment within the temptation scene itself (i.e., the angels attended to him after the forty day period), Luke drags the narratological arc down just a bit further, not as far as the Gethsemane or ascension accounts, but simply to the Nazareth episode that follows the temptation as the next main event in the Lukan storyline. In both the temptation and Nazareth episodes, Jesus is faced with the prospect of being thrown down in life-threatening ways; in the first of the two episodes, the prospect is for him to throw himself down from the Temple, while in the second, he faces the prospect of being thrown down from the Nazareth cliff. Against this backdrop, the two main episodes of Luke 4 are subtly threaded together through a Psalm that itself speaks of divinely-initiated protection ("he will command his angels concerning you, to protect you"), preserving Jesus from even dashing his "foot against a stone."

In this scenario, the narrative oddity of Luke 4:30 carries even more narrative weight for those perceptive readers or "re-

---

16. At least three scholars have already made note of the possibility: Green, *The Gospel of Luke*, 219; Schürmann, *Das Lukasevangelium*, vol. 1, 240-41; Leaney, *A Commentary on the Gospel according to St. Luke*, 51-52. Their proposals are left undeveloped, however, and are unpacked much more fully here. Complementing this prospect is the christological underpinning of allusions to Ps 91:13 in Luke 10:19, as considered in Appendix 3 below.

readers" who take note of and savor the delicate linkage of the temptation and Nazareth incidents. A christological interpretation of Ps 91:11–12 can easily bridge those two events through a narrative arc that stretches implicitly from Luke 4:10–11 to Luke 4:30.[17]

In short, Jesus' astounding deliverance in 4:30 is explained by the scriptural assurance of angelic mediation—a christological prophecy that was first articulated by the Psalmist and then temporally misapplied by Satan in his testing of Jesus in Luke 4:10–11. To assist in this linkage of the two stories, the Lukan citation of Ps 91:11, unlike its Matthean sibling, speaks of the angelic visitation as being a means "to protect you" (τοῦ διαφυλάξαι σε, Luke 4:10). That divinely-initiated angelic guarding of Jesus, foretold already in Ps 91:11, enhances the interpretation of the peculiar narrative of Luke 4:30. The narratological oddity of the Nazareth incident is so starkly drawn as to offer readers a sizeable signpost as to where the narrative arc begun in Luke 4:10–11 is to find its christological closure.

SUPPORTING THE PROPOSED CHRISTOLOGICAL ARC

If the interpretation proposed here has merit, Ps 91:11–12 is to be understood by the Gospel's audience as a christological prophecy whose fulfillment is to be found not on a Jerusalem cross, nor in a Gethsemane garden, nor above an Olivet mount; instead, its fulfillment takes place on a Nazarene cliff.[18] Six points lend

---

17. It is interesting to note that in his 1965 film *The Greatest Story Ever Told*, George Stevens links the temptation narrative with the Nazareth incident in a different fashion. After Jesus speaks of the Spirit being upon him to open the eyes of the blind, the Nazarenes bring to Jesus a blind man and charge him to work a miracle by restoring the blind man's sight. Jesus seems to prepare to work the miracle (since he knows that he can, and since he is kind), but then he draws back (knowing their unbelief), citing the words from the temptation narrative, "It is written, 'Ye shall not tempt the Lord your God.'"

18. Highlighting the interconnected dynamics within Luke 4, this proposal adds an additional attraction in placing the Nazareth incident at the forefront

Constructing Arcs

weight in support of this proposal. The fifth and sixth points will require more elaborate demonstration than the first four, which are simpler to present.

First, with his mention that Satan expected to return to test Jesus at "an opportune time" (Luke 4:13), it is clear that Luke sets up at least one narrative arc that stretches out from the temptation account to some other point in the narrative. And it is clear that a grounding-point for that arc later in the narrative is never explicitly mentioned in the plotline; if the Gethsemane account is the best candidate for the completion of that arc of Satanic testing, it is left implicit for the perceptive reader or "rereader" to discover.[19] The proposal being considered here is much the same. Consequently, the temptation account in Luke sends out not one but two narrative strands that arc over into later (and different) episodes, each one being left implicit. In each of these cases, Luke seems to expect his audience to be on the lookout for the completion point of two narrative arcs, preferring to leave those closing points tantalizingly unstated within the narrative itself.[20]

---

of Jesus' public ministry, as Luke has done. Clearly Jesus' synagogue sermon provides readers with the interpretive lens through which to interpret Jesus' ministry, making it clear why Luke has placed the Nazareth incident at the very outset of the Lukan sequencing. But an additional reason for bringing the Nazareth episode forward in the sequence of Jesus' life (at least when compared to Mark's precedent of putting it in the middle of his public career) is simply to enhance the chances of recognizing the implied arc between the two main episodes of Luke 4. Notice too the connection between this interpretation of the relationship between Luke 4:10–11/4:30 and Jesus' proclamation of "release to the captives" in Luke 4:18.

19. In my view, the perceptive scribe who inserted Luke 22:43–44 was one such reader/rereader.

20. In this light, correspondences between the first two wilderness temptations and events recounted later in Luke's Gospel become enticingly alluring. The temptation to provide bread to offset hunger in 4:1–4 might be seen to correspond to the feeding miracle of Luke 9:12–17 (compare the terminological overlap with the words "wilderness/desert" [ἔρημος] and "bread" [ἄρτος] in these two episodes), and the temptation to receive personal "glory" in 4:5–8 might be seen to correspond to 24:26 (with its emphasis on Jesus entering his "glory" only after a period of suffering).

97

Second, as Aaron Kuecker has recently demonstrated, the two episodes in Luke 4:1–13 and Luke 4:16–30 are intricately connected by the motif of Jesus' posture towards "privileged identity."[21] In both episodes, Jesus stands opposed to using his privileged identity in a centripetal manner—that is, as a means of enhancing the reputation of himself (4:1–13) or his townsfolk who expected Jesus' privileged identity to overspill to their own benefit, since he was one of them (4:16–30). Empowered by the Spirit, however, privileged identity is not to be used a means of bolstering the reputation of one's self or one's own, but is to benefit the other in need. Kuecker makes the point this way: "Privileged identity is only rightly expressed when it bears a concern for the 'other.' For Jesus, the presence of the Spirit is linked [in 4:1–13] with his personal resistance to the temptation to leverage his privileged 'Son of God' identity solely for self-benefit. This posture stands in great relief against the entitlement claims of his πατρίς ["hometown," in Luke 4:16–30], claims based upon the projection of relative prototypicality and an inappropriate understanding of privileged identity."[22] Kuecker's reading elegantly demonstrates the way in which Luke has carefully probed the literary and theological relationship between the two main episodes of Luke 4. The proposed link between 4:10–11 and 4:30 is wholly in keeping with this literary relationship.

Third, as we have seen, the theme of angelic protection gets short shrift when Psalm 91 is linked to either the ascension or the Gethsemane accounts; at no point in either of those two episodes is Jesus really in danger of dashing his foot against the rocks. This deficit is not applicable when the two main episodes of Luke 4 are read in relation to each other. Only when Ps 91:11–12 (introduced in Luke 4:10–11) is read in relation to the narrative of

---

21. See especially Kuecker, *The Spirit and the "Other,"* 72–96.
22. Ibid., 95. Kuecker's reading also makes good sense of the narrative function of the placement of Luke 4:14–15 between these two episodes, since the spread of Jesus' popularity sets up the context in which the townspeople of 4:16–30 seek to benefit from Jesus' own privileged identity.

Constructing Arcs

Luke 4:30 do the phrases "to protect you" and "so that you will not dash your foot against a stone" receive their full import.[23] No other options have that advantage.

Fourth, if a narrative arc is evident from Luke 4:10–11 to Luke 4:30, this would fall in line with a narrative tendency exhibited repeatedly by Luke in the Acts of the Apostles—that is, he leaves suprahuman characters (i.e., angels) invisible to (most of) the human characters within the story, even though the *readers* are expected to see (and are sometimes [but not always] explicitly told about) the suprahuman dimension of what is actually happening within the episodes. Evidently much the same is to be discernible within Luke 4:30.

Fifth, this reading makes sense of the pronouncement of the resurrected Jesus found near the end of Luke's Gospel: "These are my words that I spoke to you while I was still with you—that everything written about me in the law of Moses, the prophets, and the Psalms must be fulfilled (δεῖ πληρωθῆναι)" (Luke 24:44). This verse plays a key role in another Lukan *inclusio*, resonating with the phrase "the things that have been fulfilled (τῶν πεπλ-ηροφορημένων) among us" in Luke 1:1.[24] But for our purposes, it is important to note that reference to "the Psalms" is included in Jesus' statement of Luke 24:44. Nowhere else in the canonical Gospels is the motif of the fulfillment of Scripture articulated in relation to the Psalms. Common epithets when referring to the

---

23. Another Christian text takes this theme one step further. As Baarda notes ("The Flying Jesus"), the Syriac Diatessaron narrates the ending of the Nazareth episode quite differently. There, Jesus is actually thrown off the cliff but, before hitting the ground, experiences a miraculous escape, flying through the air (thereby "passing through the midst of them"?) before descending in Capernaum (Luke 4:31). I am grateful to my former research assistant, Nick Zola, for having brought this to my attention. As Zola postulates in a separate unpublished research paper, it is possible that the Diatessaron's narrative is indebted to a christological application of Ps 91:11–12 to the end of the Nazareth episode.

24. A similar *inclusio* on the theme of the fulfillment of Scripture characterizes the structure of the Acts of the Apostles. See Acts 1:16–20 and 2:16–21 in relation to Acts 28:25–28.

Hebrew Bible include "the law and the prophets" or "Moses and (all) the prophets"—phrases that Luke himself uses in Luke 16 (16:16, 29, 31) and Luke 24 (24:27). Nowhere among the canonical Gospels except at the closing of Luke's Gospel are the Psalms included in an epithet referring to the Hebrew Bible. Already in the same episode, in fact, the Hebrew Bible has been referred to without referring to the Psalms: "Then beginning with Moses and all the prophets, [Jesus] interpreted to them the things about himself in all the Scriptures" (Luke 24:27). But at the very end of Luke's Gospel, the occasion is taken to refer to the Hebrew Bible in a wholly unique manner, as the "law of Moses, the prophets, and the Psalms." Notably, then, the very end of Luke's Gospel emphasizes the theme of christological fulfillment of Scripture and, in doing so, highlights the Psalms as part of the christological matrix proffered by the Hebrew Bible.

Luke's interest in the christological fulfillment of the Psalms is evident in at least six places in his Gospel. Some of these Luke has inherited from an earlier source (either Mark's Gospel or another source), but the fourth points to the Psalms in a fashion that is distinctive to Luke's Gospel and the sixth is without precedent in any earlier sources. In sequential order, these six passages include the following:

1. Luke 3:22, where the divine voice at the baptism of Jesus speaks the words of Ps 2:7 ("You are my son; today I have begotten you"), as in Mark 1:11.

2. Luke 13:35, where Jesus cites the words of Ps 118:26 ("I tell you, you will not see me until the time comes when you say, 'Blessed is the one who comes in the name of the Lord'"), either in reliance on the source "Q" (if that lost document or oral tradition ever existed) or on Matt 23:29 (if Luke knew Matthew instead of the hypothetical "Q").

3. Luke 20:17, where Jesus recites the words of Ps 118:22 ("The stone that the builders rejected has become the cornerstone"), as in Mark 12:10–11.

4. Luke 20:42–43, where Ps 110:1 is recounted ("The Lord said to my Lord, 'Sit at my right hand, until I make your enemies your footstool'"). Although Luke has inherited this passage from Mark 12:46, it is also notable that Luke takes the occasion to point out that this passage is from "the book of Psalms," an observation that is not made in Mark's Gospel (or in Matthew's Gospel, for that matter).

5. Luke 23:34, where the soldiers casting lots to divide Jesus' clothing dramatizes Ps 22:18 ("they divide my clothes among themselves and for my clothing they cast lots"), as in Mark 15:24.

6. Luke 23:46, where Jesus recites the words of Ps 31:5 ("Into your hand I commit my spirit"), without precedent in Mark's Gospel.

It is not too much to think that we should add a seventh passage in this assembly of texts that fall under the rubric of "everything written about me in . . . the Psalms" that "must be fulfilled"—i.e., Ps 91:11–12, fulfilled in Luke 4:30.

Sixth (and this point will take some paragraphs to demonstrate), like any good storyteller, Luke has a tendency to group things together that are most profitably to be read alongside of and in relation to each other. Some cases are more evident than others. For instance, the technique of grouping separate episodes together in order that they might be interpreted in relation to each other is clearly evident in Luke 15. There the parable of the lost sheep (15:1–7; cf. Matt 18:12–14) is linked to the parable of the lost coin (15:8–10; without parallel in the other Gospels) and the parable of the lost son (15:11–32; without parallel in the other Gospels).[25] The theme of recovering something precious that had been lost weaves its way through those parables in an obvious fashion.

---

25. The Greek verb ἀπόλλυμι appears with the sense "to lose" in 15:4, 6, 8–9, 24, 32, and appears in 15:17 on the lips of the "prodigal son" with the sense "to perish" ("I am dying").

At times, however, Luke links two episodes side-by-side in a much more subtle manner. This is the case, for instance, in the early part of Luke 5. In Luke 5:1–11, the miraculous catch of fish is recounted, followed in 5:12–16 with the account of Jesus healing a leper. Although similarities may not be evident at first blush, on further consideration, there are significant points of interplay between these two stories. In each, the main protagonist (apart from Jesus himself) responds to Jesus in identical ways. So in the first account, we are shown Peter's response to the miraculous catch of fish (5:8): "When Simon Peter saw it (ἰδών), he fell down (προσέπεσεν) at Jesus' knees, saying, 'Go away from me, Lord (κύριε), for I am a sinful man!'" This threefold pattern of seeing, falling prostrate before Jesus, and referring to Jesus as "Lord/lord" is then repeated in the account of the leper's healing: When the man covered with leprosy "saw (ἰδών) Jesus, he bowed (πεσών) with his face to the ground and begged him, 'Lord (κύριε), if you choose, you can make me clean.'" As Kavin Rowe has argued, when these two stories are placed back-to-back, the audience is predisposed to read the second episode in light of the first. In the process, Peter's highly theological acclamation of Jesus as "Lord" (κύριε) in contrast to sinful men is expected to reverberate within the leper's own acclamation of Jesus as "Lord" (κύριε), even if the audience is seeing more to the leper's designation of Jesus than the leper himself might have intended (perhaps meaning only "sir"). Although the audience is not explicitly directed to notice the relationship of these two episodes, "the immediate proximity of the two pericopae can hardly be taken as accidental," with the second intended to be interpreted in light of the first.[26]

Another example of subtle interconnectivity between neighboring episodes is likely to be evident in Luke 10:25–42. In the first episode of this section, Jesus engages in a dialogue with a "lawyer" about how to inherit eternal life. Both Jesus and the lawyer agree that eternal life involves loving "the Lord your God with

---

26. Rowe, *Early Narrative Christology*, 90.

Constructing Arcs

all your heart, and with all your soul, and with all your strength, and with all your mind; and your neighbor as yourself." When the lawyer probes further to ask "who is my neighbor" (10:29), Jesus responds by narrating the parable of the Good Samaritan (10:30–37). The second episode in this section recounts Jesus visiting the house of Mary and Martha (10:38–42). In that account, Mary sits at his feet and listens to the voice of her "lord" while Martha is busy with preparations; upon Martha's protestations, Mary is praised by Jesus but Martha is gently rebuked: "Martha, Martha, you are worried and distracted by many things; there is need of only one thing. Mary has chosen the better part, which will not be taken away from her."

Although there is no explicit linking of these two episodes within Luke's Gospel, it is likely that they are not simply to be read as distinct and unrelated events. Instead, the second is to be read in relation to the first. Placed alongside of each other, these two episodes sit in what initially appears to be a position of tension to each other. That tension is raised when Martha asks Jesus the poignant and reasonable question, "do you not care that my sister has left me to do all the work by myself?" Following on from the parable of the Good Samaritan, Martha's question is augmented in its poignancy. John R. Donahue makes the point well: "having just been given in the Samaritan an example of active concern for another, readers might expect Jesus to urge Mary to help her sister."[27] Of course, Jesus does precisely the opposite.

But the reader is not expected to scratch her head at the curious combination of episodes. Instead, by means of the narrative oddity of putting two episodes back to back that seem to emphasize contrasting things, the reader is invited to "ponder anew" how this episodic curiosity might be explained.

The key to this puzzle is likely to be found in Luke 10:27, during the exchange between Jesus and the lawyer. In Mark's account of this exchange (Mark 12:28–31), Jesus and the lawyer agree that eternal life emerges from the observance of two com-

---

27. Donahue, *The Gospel in Parable*, 136–37.

mandments: (1) "you shall love of the Lord your God," and (2) "you shall love your neighbor as yourself." That these are two commandments is reinforced by Jesus' comment in Mark "There is no other commandment greater than these [two]." In Luke's account, however, the two commandments appear as one commandment with a double aspect to it: "You shall love (1) the Lord your God with all your heart, and with all your soul, and with all your strength, and with all your mind; and (2) your neighbor as yourself." What we find in the parable of the Good Samaritan who cares for the half-dead man along the wayside is an elaboration of the second component of the single commandment ("love your neighbor as yourself"). What we find in the story of Jesus with Mary and Martha is an elaboration of the first component of the single commandment ("love the Lord your God"); elaborated in story form, that dimension of the single commandment is portrayed as listening to the "lord" Jesus in a posture of discipleship, like that of Mary.

In other words, something greater than the sum of their parts emerges when these two episodes are placed alongside each other and under the single banner of the commandment to love God and neighbor. The commandment to "love the Lord your God . . . and your neighbor as yourself" links through the explicit question, "who is my neighbor?" to the parable of the Good Samaritan and, through the implicit question "who is the Lord our God?," to the narrative of Jesus the "lord/Lord" with Mary and Martha. In the process, a sermonic narrative about the multi-dimensional character of love emerges, highlighting the way that a balanced "love" involves the mutual interpenetration of both compassionate service to others and careful attentiveness to God. In this way, the parable of the Good Samaritan and the episode of Jesus with Mary and Martha function as two parts of a diptych that Luke leaves for his readers (or rereaders) to discover.[28]

28. Compare Donahue (ibid., 136–38): "The parable of the Good Samaritan with its exhortation to do mercy to the neighbor and the story of Martha and

Although this sixth point might appear to have taken us on a long diversion, in fact it has done the opposite. It has demonstrated Luke's penchant for linking episodes back-to-back so that the audience will recognize literary and theological features between them. Those features, while unstated and implicit, are nonetheless notable and rewarding for audiences who, perhaps on a "rereading" of the material, begin to notice the theological interpenetration of neighboring episodes that characterizes so much of Luke's Gospel.

THEOLOGY THROUGH LITERARY ARTISTRY

It was proposed above that the temptation and Nazareth episodes have been placed side-by-side in order to permit an unarticulated link to emerge between them, through the christological fulfillment of Psalm 91 stretching implicitly from Luke 4:10–11 to Luke 4:30. And we have seen reason to think that this proposal falls in line with the way that Luke constructs his storyline in general. If this line of thinking has merit, it demonstrates the subtle ways in which Luke has finessed his storyline in order to embed within it features that are left for the audience to discover. This discovery is unlikely to have emerged from a first hearing of Luke's Gospel—the subtlety is perhaps too thin for that. But Luke may have hoped that the delicate linkage could be discovered on subsequent encounters with the Gospel narrative, when better

---

Mary with its praise of the one who sits and listens to the Lord form a twofold parabolic illustration of the single command . . . To love God with whole heart and mind and the neighbor as one's self demands both compassionate and effective entry into the world of the neighbor as well as undistracted attentiveness to the word of the Lord. Far from exalting one mode of discipleship above the other, the two narratives say that one cannot authentically exist without the other . . . The Good Samaritan is the one who 'does' mercy to the injured man . . . Conversely, Mary is the one who 'keeps listening' . . . while the 'doing' of Martha is rejected. Each parabolic narrative portrays the danger of separating 'doing' and 'hearing'; taken together, they offer an inseparable vignette of the way of discipleship. Following Jesus on the way involves compassion for the suffering neighbor and attention to the word of God."

familiarity would allow his audience to put pieces of the literary puzzle together in a constructive fashion.

Something similar has been proposed by Richard Bauckham regarding the intricate artistry "on display" in the text of Revelation. Bauckham demonstrates the existence of several complex features in that text, such as (1) the seven-fold repetition of numerous themes, phrases, or terms throughout the narrative, (2) the incorporation of numbers that carry meaning beyond their "surface function" (i.e., the function of square, rectangular, and triangular numbers), and (3) subtle intratextual linkages spread through the narrative.[29] Notable features such as these add to the artistic and theological dimensions of the narrative without explicit instruction as to their presence or their interpretive significance. The work of discovery and of interpretation is left to the auditors to perform. So, according to Bauckham,

> Revelation was evidently designed to convey its message to some significant degree on first hearing (cf. 1:3), but also progressively to yield fuller meaning to closer acquaintance and assiduous study. [The author of Revelation] was writing a book which he intended to have a status comparable to the Old Testament prophetic books, and he could expect some readers to study it with the same intensity with which he himself studied Old Testament prophetic books. His work would convey sufficient meaning in oral performance in the worship meetings of the churches of Asia, but it would also have much more to offer those . . . who pondered it with prayerful and scripturally learned attention.[30]

29. Bauckham, *The Climax of Prophecy*. On the first and third, see the chapter "Structure and Composition," and for the second, see his chapter "Nero and the Beast."

30. Ibid., 1, 30. Bauckham goes on to note that, in the circumstances of ancient composition, this level of textual artistry "would not have been easy to achieve. It is further evidence of the meticulous composition of the book . . . We could say that he buried in the literary composition of his work theological significance which few readers have subsequently unearthed, though it may well be that, among his first readers, at least his fellow-prophets would know better than later readers what to look for" (ibid., 33).

Constructing Arcs

Bauckham proposes that complex literary features were intentionally placed within the narrative of Revelation so that attentive auditors might catch these links not so much on a first encounter with the text but at some point in subsequent readings, being little gold nuggets for edification as the auditors' familiarity with the text grows.

Here we can recall Wolfgang Iser's description whereby readers construct meaning from a text: "we look forward, we look back, we decide, we change our decisions, we form expectations, we are shocked by their nonfulfillment, we question, we muse, we accept, we reject."[31] The alert and engaged audience is constantly involved in the process of anticipating what might follow in the narrative and of reviewing what has already taken place, all the while being open to reevaluating their impressions and interpretations to better coincide with the text's "norms and directives."

Perhaps something similar is to take place for audiences of Luke's Gospel with regard to the christological fulfillment of Psalm 91. Once a certain level of familiarity with Luke's Gospel is reached, it is only a matter of time (for reasons outlined earlier in this chapter) before the link between Luke 4:10–11 and Luke 4:30 is considered. When that penny drops, the audience is treated to a discovery of further literary and theological dimensions of a text with which they have already become well familiar, with familiarity breeding not contempt but alluring novelties.

DROPPING PENNIES

At this point, late in the argumentation of this book, one final matter must be raised. If the proposal entertained in this chapter has cogency within "the givens of the text," why does it have such a humble presence within the annals of Lukan interpretation? Shouldn't we expect interpretative cogency be tied to the frequency of advocacy, with infrequent advocacy inevitably telling

---

31. Iser, "The Reading Process," 293.

against cogency? Should we at this point speak less of cogency in relation to the text's "norms and directives" and speak more about adopting simply a "playful reading" of the text? While that option must always be given due consideration, it is nonetheless the case that the sound of dropping pennies has at times been heard in the house of Lukan interpretation in relation to the main proposal of this chapter. For instance, three responsible and respected interpreters of Luke's Gospel have supported the proposal within the last few generations of scholarship (although their consideration of the matter has been relatively unadorned with supporting argumentation): Joel Green (1997), Heinz Schürmann (1969), and Alfred Leaney (1958).[32] Perhaps an intentional study of "reception history" would reveal other moments of interpretive history in which the penny has dropped among "credentialed" interpreters.

But two other indicators also encourage me to think that the penny is, in a sense, poised to drop for interpreters primed to recognize the eucatastrophe within Luke 4:30, the first indicator being anecdotal, and the second arising from a Jesus-novel.

First, about a month before sending the manuscript of this book to the publisher, I presented the core ideas of this book in two public lectures at North Park Theological Seminary in Chicago.[33] The first lecture dealt with the narrative gap of Luke 4:30, and in that lecture I presented the case for seeing the gap

---

32. Green, *The Gospel of Luke*, 219 ("The nature of Jesus' escape from the violent mob bent on stoning him is not developed, though one may hear in the background reverberations of the divine promise misapplied by the devil in 4.10-11"); Schürmann, *Das Lukasevangelium*, vol. 1, 240-41 ("Der Psalm 91,11 verheissene wunderbare Schutz, den herauszufordern 4,12 satanische Versuchung war, wird hier im rechten Augenblick dem Bedrängten gewährt"). Cf. Leaney, *The Gospel according to St. Luke*, 51-52 ("the hint of the angelic protection which is brought near the end of that [temptation] narrative may be connected with the fact that Jesus escapes with mysterious lack of effort when threatened at iv.29"). Leaney's comments on p. 120 go disastrously wrong, however, when he confusingly (and confusedly) writes: "he [Jesus] here escapes a death by being dashed against rock with apparently supernatural ease."

33. The Nils Lund Lectures (September 29, 2011).

Constructing Arcs

as a "eucatastrophic" moment in the Lukan narrative. At the end of the lecture, members of the audience wanted to reflect on the possible mechanisms of eucatastrophe—that is, they wanted to consider what particular *form* divine involvement took in the gap of Luke 4:30. Someone proposed that the resources for divine eucatastrophe emerged from Jesus himself, while someone else proposed that eucatastrophe was orchestrated through the involvement of the Spirit. While giving full consideration to the potential of each of these suggestions, I nonetheless kept my cards close to my chest, and my powder dry, waiting to reveal an alternative suggestion in the next lecture, where the arc between Luke 4:10–11 and Luke 4:30 would be proposed. During the coffee break between those two lectures (and as I was later to learn), one of the faculty members who had attended the first lecture proposed to others with whom he was having coffee that we need to consider whether the eucatastrophe arises through angelic instrumentality, in fulfillment of Psalm 91, already recited in the temptation narrative.

What happened in this instance? Quite simply, having been introduced to the important theological function of the narrative gap of Luke 4:30, an interpreter who had been attuned to matters of eucatastrophe in that verse immediately considered whether a christological interpretation of Ps 91:11–12 might hold the key to hearing the silence of Luke 4:30. That is, once an interpreter is sensitive to the eucatastrophic significance of Luke 4:30, the penny is readied to drop and, as in this particular instance, sometimes does.

A second example is less anecdotal, but demonstrates much the same thing, arising from the world of Jesus-novels. As was noted in chapter 5, Michael Monhollon's novel *Divine Invasion* depicts Jesus' deliverance from the clutches of his townspeople in Luke 4:30 as having been effected by means of divine initiative.[34] Monhollon's Jesus himself articulates the point. When subsequently reflecting on his deliverance from the people of

---

34. Monhollon, *Divine Invasion*, 60–61.

Nazareth, Jesus provocatively asks his disciples, "Are you more ready to believe in [a natural cause-and-effect explanation for the event] or in God's providence?" Here a eucatastrophic analysis of Luke 4:30 emerges from the mouth of Monhollon's Jesus. But a further dimension of eucatastrophic analysis is also advocated by Monhollon's Jesus. In fact, for Monhollon, the eucatastrophe of that verse is unpacked further in relation to angelic instrumentality. So, Jesus' release occurs through the appearance of an angel, with all of the human characters in the Nazareth incident falling to the ground and being temporarily blinded by a dazzling (angelic) light. Further still, in the Monhollon novel this angelic instrumentality is linked to the fulfillment of Ps 91:11–12, although in an extremely subtle fashion, with the link between the events of Luke 4:10–11 and Luke 4:30 being left for only the attentive reader to notice. So, departing from Nazareth Jesus discusses with Simon Peter what happened there. Jesus recites Ps 91:11–12 to Simon Peter and says to him, "I've had the passage quoted to me recently, in another context." When Simon Peter asks, "What context?" Jesus retorts, "I'll tell you later, when you're ready to hear it." In Monhollon's handling, the informed reader (as opposed to Peter) knows that the "context" in which Psalm 91 had already been quoted to Jesus is the temptation account in which Satan tested him with the words of Ps 91:11–12. What Monhollon has constructed, then, is a very subtle and unarticulated linkage between the Nazareth incident and Jesus' temptation, with Ps 91:11–12 having its christological fulfillment not at the pinnacle of the temple, as proposed by Satan, but at the top of a cliff in Nazareth.

So it seems that the penny has, in fact, dropped at times, at least in recent years. This is true of a few academic scholars, of course. But it is also true of a few "ordinary" readers of Gospel narratives who, when sensitized to the prospect of eucatastrophe within Luke 4:30, subsequently identify the events of Luke 4:30 as the second point in an arc stretching back to Luke 4:10–11. If this chapter's main proposal requires precedent within the annals

Constructing Arcs

of interpretive history in order to be given serious consideration, there is at least a modicum of "reception history" to give it a foothold, should the norms and directives of the text be seen to permit it.

APPENDIX
ONE

Narrations of Acts 14:19–20

It was noted in chapter 4 above[1] that the events of Acts 14:19–20 (i.e., Paul's stoning and notable recovery) offer some parallels to the events of Luke 4:28–30 (Jesus in the grip of an enraged mob but slipping through their midst). Here we focus on the manner in which the Paul episode has been narrated by novelists.

Novelists go in two different directions when fictionalizing the event. Some heighten the sense of oddity and the involvement of divine initiative, while others remove the oddity and steer clear of the possibility of divine initiative. Curiously, both approaches are taken by conservative novelists. Representing the second approach (i.e., Paul's recovery results from normal cause-and-effect relationships), the conservative novelist John Pollock narrates the incident in this way in his novel *The Apostle*:

> A youth picked up a stone, took aim and with a vicious flick caught Paul full face. In a moment, before Barnabas or his friends could protect him, he was under a shower of stones, on his jaw, the pit of his stomach, his groin, his chest, his temple. He fell stark and stiff, blood streaming from nose and eyes. The crowd dragged the body out

---

1. Specifically in the sub-section entitled "Comparing Incidents of Divine Causality."

APPENDIX ONE

of the city and melted quickly away before the Roman guards at the gate could identify individual murderers.

Converts who had watched, appalled at the sudden assault, formed a ring round the body, shocked and uncertain.

Paul stirred. With every muscle and nerve seared, head throbbing, stomach retching, he forced himself to stand.

They helped him slowly through streets empty because the mob lay low for fear of civic action. They dressed his wounds but it was not safe to stay more than a night. The next day, when every bone in his body cried out to rest, he set off with Barnabas [on a trip that Pollock describes as "torture" for Paul].[2]

There is not a trace of divine involvement in Pollock's narrative. Virtually the same elements are evident in James Cannon's *Apostle Paul*.[3] These conservative novels depict cause-and-effect relationships devoid of superhuman involvement, since Paul was just "lucky" to get away with his life intact. But a theology of luck falls far short of the theological program that Luke seems to envision.

A similar storyline for Acts 14:19–20 is constructed by Bruce Chilton in his pseudo-narrative *Rabbi Paul*: "[The Jews who stirred up trouble] seized Paul from the house he was staying in and took him to a cliff. Stripping him naked, they threw him off and crushed him with a huge stone. A few smaller rocks gashed his inert flesh. In Lystra, his enemies left Paul for dead." Then Chilton shifts from narration to explication. "Paul was not in any shape to travel. In an interlude that would be comic were it intentional, Acts has him just pick himself up after the stoning to retrace his steps with Barnabas through the same places where people had all but killed him (Acts 14:20–21). That strains credibility to the breaking point and betrays the strong tendency toward legendary embellishment in Acts."

2. Pollock, *The Apostle*, 70–71.
3. Cannon, *Apostle Paul*, 241.

Narrations of Acts 14:19-20

Notice Chilton's certainty that the narrative "strains credibility to the breaking point" and "would be comic" if it were "intentional." Apart from a "eucatastrophic perspective," the storyline needs to be filled with cause-and-effect relationships of another kind. Accordingly, Chilton narrates events in this way: "[S]ympathizers circled around him . . . crying prayers and lamentations as they lifted his broken body from the ground. A circle of healing answered the executioners' circle of stoning . . . They brought him to Derbe . . . Had he died there, it would have been near his home. But he did not die. He revived under care—treatment, rest, and nutrition as well as prayer."[4]

Something of the same order is found in James Dunn's *Beginning in Jerusalem*: "Luke's report that Paul was able immediately to return to the city . . . and on the very next day to undertake the demanding journey to Derbe inevitably causes some eyebrow raising. Luke was evidently cutting several corners and for some reason chose not to make much at all of the severity of Paul's sufferings."[5] In all this common sense, there isn't a shred of an implicit divine involvement; just Luke "cutting narrative corners."

An interpretation similar to the "athletic dodge" has been proposed by Stephen Chapman, although in this case in relation to Paul's own physical condition. Noting how Paul survives a shipwreck and a snakebite in Acts 27–28, Chapman imagines that Paul's "survival could thus imply a person who is at least fairly hale and hardy, if not also big and strong."[6] But within its

---

4. Chilton, *Rabbi Paul*, 123-25.
5. Dunn, *Beginning from Jerusalem*, 433. Cf. Gaventa, *Acts*, 208: "Luke is more concerned with demonstrating the intensity of persecution and the concern of Paul's fellow-believers than he is with verisimilitude, and a number of details drop by the wayside. For example, how is it the disciples know that Paul is alive and the crowd does not? How does the apparently dead Paul rise and reenter the city without precipitating further persecution? And how is he capable of travelling on the following day?"
6. Chapman, "Saul/Paul," 225.

narrative context, Paul's "survival" is most likely suggestive of divine involvement.

In contrast to those listed above, it is Walter Wangerin who narrates Acts 14:19–20 in terms of a theology of divine involvement. In his book *Paul: A Novel*, he repeatedly depicts the lifelessness of Paul's body in this incident. Here, for instance, Barnabas speaks: "They were stoning Saul! I heard the crack of stones on the street. I heard the punch of the stones on his body . . . I watched him stiffen under the storm. I saw him fold into himself. Then he sighed and went slack. One great rock bounced off his head, but he didn't move, neither twitched nor shivered. He had become a broken doll on the dark street. Men grabbed his arms and dragged him away." Barnabas likens Paul to a lamb, "struck once with a mallet in the centre of its skull, dropped and was instantly dead. Plainly dead. There was no recovery, then." When Barnabas and others go to find Paul's body, it is lying crumpled in the ditch, in a position suitable only for discarded corpses, with "his legs doubled beneath him, his arms flopped over his face." When Barnabas whispers "We'll carry him home" and begins to cry, the discarded corpse says, "Oh, Barnabas; that's silly." A moment later Paul "climbed from the ditch and stood up and said, 'Come on,' and began to walk back to the city" at a quick pace.[7] The miraculous is clearly being depicted here in relation to Paul's experiences of Acts 14:19–20. But this makes for an extremely curious situation, since Wangerin adopts the "athletic dodge" explanation for Jesus in Luke 4:30, without entertaining the possibility of divine involvement in that episode. One might expect Wangerin to have entertained a similar kind of suprahuman causality when depicting Jesus' situation in Luke 4:28–30 as he had already entertained when depicting Paul's situation in Acts 14:19–20.

---

7. Wangerin, *Paul*, 108-9.

APPENDIX
TWO

What If Luke 22:43-44 Is Original to Luke's Gospel?

IN CHAPTER 7 ABOVE, an argument was made for seeing Ps 91:11-12 as implicitly fulfilled christologically in the events of Luke 4:30. And it was postulated that a later scribe had inserted Luke 22:43-44 into the Lukan narrative in order to ensure that Ps 91:11-12 is seen to be fulfilled at that point in the narrative. But it needs to be asked, What are the implications for the argument of chapter 7 if Luke 22:43-44 is not a later scribal insertion but is, instead, original to the Lukan Gospel, as a minority of scholars believe?

In that case, the argument of chapter 7 may require some reconsideration (even if the argument of the first six chapters does not). In an "either-or" scenario, if Ps 91:11-12 is fulfilled in Luke 22:43-44, then it is not fulfilled in Luke 4:30.

There are, however, two scenarios that circumvent this, even on the assumption that Luke 22:43-44 is original to Luke's Gospel. The first scenario steers clear of an "either-or" formulation, while the second builds upon it. First, it was proposed in chapter 4 that an *inclusio* encapsulates the beginning and ending of Jesus' public ministry in Luke's Gospel, with divine intervention characterizing the first recounted episode of Jesus' ministry (the Nazareth incident) and the resurrection. If Luke 22:43-44 is original to Luke's Gospel, and if christological fulfillment of Ps 91:11–12 is evident there, it need not be assumed that Ps 91:11–12 is fulfilled solely in that late event; recognizing the "bookending" that characterizes much of Luke's structuring technique enables us to see Ps 91:11–12 as having its fulfillment in a double-aspect bookending, toward the start of Jesus' public ministry in 4:30 and toward the end of that ministry in 22:43–44. Luke's fondness for *inclusio* permits precisely this possibility.

Second, it may be the case that Luke 22:43–44 is original but does not represent the fulfillment of Ps 91:11–12. After all, while there is angelic "protection" of Jesus in the garden episode, there is no sense in which Jesus' feet are in danger of being dashed against the rocks, as explicitly mentioned in the Psalm. It is only in Luke 4:30 that we find a situation in which an angelic protection pertains to the danger of Jesus' feet being dashed against the rocks. Moreover, the Lukan penchant for implicitly linking episodes side-by-side so that they interpret each other in some fashion coincides with this view. And, as Aaron Kuecker has demonstrated, the two main episodes of Luke 4 link together in terms of their import regarding privileged identity. Consequently, if Luke 22:43–44 is original, and if we are to think in "either-or" terms, it is easier to recognize the christological fulfillment of Ps 91:11–12 in the events of Luke 4:30 than in those of 22:43–44.

Four scenarios are possible:

1. Luke 22:43–44 is not original to the text of Luke's Gospel, and Ps 91:11–12 is fulfilled only in the events of Luke 4:30;

2. Luke 22:43–44 is original to the text of Luke's Gospel, and Ps 91:11–12 is fulfilled only in the events of Luke 4:30;

3. Luke 22:43–44 is original to the text of Luke's Gospel, and Ps 91:11–12 is fulfilled in the events of *both* Luke 4:30 *and* Luke 22:43–44;

4. Luke 22:43–44 is original to the text of Luke's Gospel, and Ps 91:11–12 is fulfilled only in the events of Luke 22:43–44.

What If Luke 22:43–44 Is Original to Luke's Gospel?

In my view, for reasons outlined above, the enumeration of these four also reflects their likelihood (with "1" reflecting the most likely and "4" reflecting the least likely scenario).

APPENDIX THREE

Luke's Christological Interpretation of Psalm 91:3

EVIDENCE WITHIN THE LUKAN Gospel lends support to the view that Luke interprets Ps 91:11-12 christologically. At one point, in fact, Ps 91:13 shapes Luke's narrative and illustrates a christological underpinning of the Psalm in the process.

To see this most clearly, it will be helpful to set out a structural outline of the Lukan travel section (Luke 9:51 to 21:38)—a Lukan narrative in which Jesus travels to Jerusalem in the presence of followers. Roland Meynet argues that the travel section of Luke's Gospel comprises three main subsections, the first of which is 9:51—13:21. That section itself comprises three parts, the first of which is contained in 9:51—10:42 (i.e., "Jesus Undertakes His Journey to Jerusalem"). That section itself is constructed, Meynet argues, in chiastic fashion, as follows:

Section A: 9:51–56
Section B: 9:57—10:11
Section C: 10:12–16
Section D: 10:17–20
Section C^1: 10:21–24
Section B^1: 10:25–37
Section A^1: 10:38–42

Luke's Christological Interpretation of Psalm 91:3

In structured chiasm of this sort, the centerpiece is normally to carry significant interpretive weight. The chiastic center for this subsection is section D, comprising Luke 10:17–20, in which Jesus gives seventy(-two) of his followers the power over Jesus' suprahuman opponent and his opponent's entourage (cf. Luke 9:1). The passage is as follows:

> The seventy returned with joy, saying, "Lord, in your name even the demons submit to us!" He said to them, "I watched Satan fall from heaven like a flash of lightning. See, I have given you authority to tread on snakes and scorpions, and over all the power of the enemy; and nothing will hurt you. Nevertheless, do not rejoice at this, that the spirits submit to you, but rejoice that your names are written in heaven."

Echoes of Psalm 91 resound at the center of this section—i.e., the very heart of the section that bears the interpretive weight of the passages surrounding it.[1] In Luke 10:19 Jesus says that the disciples have been given "authority to tread (πατέω) on snakes and scorpions, and over the power of the enemy; and nothing will hurt you." The scriptural passage of Ps 91:13 (90:13 in LXX) says "You will squash the asp and the serpent, and you will tread on (καταπατέω) the lion and the dragon." The thought pattern is shared, even though the same is not always the case for specific points of terminology. In the Lukan narrative, for instance, there is no mention of a "lion," and the imagery of the "adder" and the "serpent" in the Psalms appears in Luke as "snakes and scorpions." But Luke's narrative interests may go some way in explaining the terminological differences, precisely in an effort to link the narrative of his Gospel to the (subsequent) narrative of his Acts of the Apostles. For in the subsequent volume of Acts, Paul is bitten by a viper but tosses it off into the fire, being unharmed (Acts 28:1–6). Jesus' promise that his followers will remain unhurt by snakes in Luke 10:19 has its narrative fulfillment

---

1. Meynet, *L'Évangile selon saint Luc*, 491: "Ps 91,13 est cité au centre du text."

in Acts 28, where the promise "nothing will hurt you" in Luke 10:19 is matched by "he suffered no harm" of Acts 28:5. With his eyes already on the narrative of Acts, Luke seems to allude to Ps 91:13 in Luke 10:19, even though he adjusts the terminology of the allusion slightly in order to create an implicit link between Jesus' commissioning of his disciples and an episode in Paul's life towards the end of Acts.

The real thing to note about Luke 10:19, however, is that this subjugation of Jesus' suprahuman enemy (i.e., Satan) is not carried out primarily or exclusively in the ministry of Jesus' seventy(-two) followers (and by implication, by the church of Acts). Behind the ministry of these followers we are to recognize the empowerment of Jesus' own activity. That is, theologically speaking Luke 10:17–20 points first of all to the narrative of Jesus' crucifixion and resurrection in Luke 22–24; only in relation to *that* narrative do the narratives of Jesus' followers emerge.

This is especially clear from Meynet's outline. In a section dealing with Jesus setting out on his journey to Jerusalem (i.e., 9:51—10:42), the center of that chiastic section sets up the ministry of the seventy(-two) as the interpretive lens for understanding what Jesus intends to accomplish by going to Jerusalem. The ministry of Jesus' followers is, in a sense, a miniature version of aspects of Jesus' own life-giving ministry. It is in Jesus' life, death, and resurrection that Satan's influence is ultimately overthrown, involving the treading on metaphorical snakes and scorpions, the breaking of the enemy's power, the submission of the powers of evil. Luke has structured his material so that the commissioning of the disciples falls within the programmatic section that outlines Jesus' intention to journey to Jerusalem (where he must go "because it is impossible for a prophet to be killed outside of Jerusalem," 13:33). In this way, a christological interpretation lies behind the allusions to Ps 91:13 in Luke 10:19. If Ps 91:13 is applied to the disciples in Luke 10:19, beyond that there lies an even grander application of the Psalm in the ministry of Jesus, accomplished in Jerusalem, where he has now set his face. A

Luke's Christological Interpretation of Psalm 91:3

non-christological application of Ps 91:13 in Luke 10:19 is ultimately driven, then, by a christological interpretation of that same verse. With this interpretive frame in place at the start of the Lukan travel narrative, Luke leaves his audience to spot its implications for interpreting Jesus' own death and resurrection, as recounted later in the Lukan narrative without the necessary gestures to Ps 91:13.

The point for our purposes is that Luke seems ultimately to understand Ps 91:13 christologically, just as he seems to interpret Ps 91:11–12 christologically in the manner proposed in chapter 7 above.

Bibliography

Alter, Robert. *The Pleasures of Reading in an Ideological Age*. New York: Simon and Schuster, 1989.
Appleby, Joyce Oldham, Lynn Hunt, and Margaret Jacob. *Telling the Truth about History*. New York: Norton, 1994.
Archer, Jeffrey. *The Gospel according to Judas, by Benjamin Iscariot*. London: Macmillan, 2007.
Asch, Sholem. *The Nazarene*. New York: Putnam's Sons, 1939.
Baarda, Tjitze. "'The Flying Jesus': Luke 4:29–30 in the Syriac Diatessaron." *Vigiliae Christianae* 40 (1986) 313–41.
Barclay, William. *Jesus of Nazareth*. London: Collins, 1977.
Barthes, Roland. "The Death of the Author." In *Image, Music, Text*, edited by S. Heath, 142–48. New York: Hill and Wang, 1977.
Bauckham, Richard, ed. *Gospels for All Christians: Rethinking the Gospel Audiences*. Grand Rapids: Eerdmans, 1998.
Bauckham, Richard. *The Climax of Prophecy: Studies on the Book of Revelation*. Edinburgh: T. & T. Clark, 1993.
Beavis, Mary Ann L. "The Trial before the Sanhedrin (Mark 14:53–65): Reader Response and Greco-Roman Readers." *Catholic Biblical Quarterly* 49 (1987) 581–96.
The Bible and Culture Collective. *The Postmodern Bible*. New Haven: Yale University Press, 1995.
Boring, M. Eugene. *Mark*. Louisville: Westminster John Knox, 2006.
Boyd, Neil. *The Hidden Years: A Novel about Jesus*. London: Hodder and Stoughton, 1984.
Brown, Raymond E. *The Death of the Messiah: From Gethsemane to the Grave*. New York: Doubleday, 1994.
Bultmann, Rudolf. "Is Exegesis without Presuppositions Possible?" In *Existence and Faith: The Shorter Writings of Rudolf Bultmann*, translated by Schubert M. Ogden, 289–96. New York: Meridian, 1960.
Campbell, Douglas A. "An Attempt to be Understood: A Response to the Concerns of Matlock and Macaskill with *The Deliverance of God*." *Journal for the Study of the New Testament*, forthcoming.
Cannon, James. *Apostle Paul*. Hanover, NH: Steerforth, 2005.

Bibliography

Chapman, Stephen B. "Saul/Paul: Onomastics, Typology, and Christian Scripture." In *The Word Leaps the Gap: Essays on Scripture and Theology in Honor of Richard B. Hays*, edited by J. Ross Wagner, C. Kavin Rowe, and A. Katherine Grieb, 214-43. Grand Rapids: Eerdmans, 2008.

Chilton, Bruce. *Rabbi Jesus: An Intimate Biography*. New York: Image, 2000.

―――. *Rabbi Paul*. New York: Doubleday, 2004.

Clivaz, Claire. *L'Ange et la sueur de sang (Lc 22, 43-44) ou comment on pourrait bien encore écrire l'histoire*. Leuven: Peeters, 2010.

―――. "The Angel and the Sweat Like 'Drops of Blood' (Lk 22:43-44): P69 and f13." *Harvard Theological Review* 98 (2005) 419-40.

Coleridge, Mark. *The Birth of the Lukan Narrative: Narrative as Christology in Luke 1-2*. Sheffield, UK: Sheffield Academic Press, 1994.

Culy, Martin C., Mikeal C. Parsons, and Joshua J. Stigall. *Luke: A Handbook on the Greek Text*. Waco, TX: Baylor University Press, 2010.

Cunningham, Scott. *"Through Many Tribulations": The Theology of Persecution in Luke-Acts*. Sheffield, UK: Sheffield Academic Press, 1997.

Cyril of Alexandria. *A Commentary upon the Gospel according to S. Luke, by S. Cyril, Patriarch of Alexandria*, Part 1. Translated by R. Payne Smith. Oxford: Oxford University Press, 1859.

Donahue, John R. *The Gospel in Parable: Metaphor, Narrative, and Theology in the Synoptic Gospels*. Minneapolis: Fortress, 1988.

Dunn, James D. G. *Beginning from Jerusalem: Christianity in the Making*, vol. 2. Grand Rapids: Eerdmans, 2007.

Ehrman, Bart D. *Misquoting Jesus: The Story behind Who Changed the Bible and Why*. San Francisco: HarperSanFrancisco, 2005.

Esler, Philip F. *New Testament Theology: Communion and Community*. Minneapolis: Fortress, 2005.

Evans, Craig A. "Luke's Use of the Elijah/Elisha Narratives and the Ethics of Election." *Journal of Biblical Literature* 106 (1987) 75-83.

Fish, Stanley E. *Is There a Text in This Class? The Authority of Interpretive Communities*. Cambridge: Cambridge University Press, 1980.

Fisk, Bruce N. "See My Tears: A Lament for Jerusalem (Luke 13:31-35; 19:41-44)." In *The Word Leaps the Gap: Essays on Scripture and Theology in Honor of Richard B. Hays*, edited by J. Ross Wagner, C. Kavin Rowe, and A. Katherine Grieb, 147-78. Grand Rapids: Eerdmans, 2008.

Fitzmyer, Joseph A. *The Gospel according to Luke*, vol. 1. Garden City, NY: Doubleday, 1981.

Flynn, Elizabeth A., and Patrocinio P. Schweickart, eds. *Gender and Reading: Essays on Readers, Texts, and Contents*. Baltimore: Johns Hopkins University Press, 1986.

Fortney, Steven. *The Thomas Jesus*. Oregon, WI: Waubesa, 2000.

Freke, Timothy, and Peter Gandy. *The Gospel of the Second Coming*. London: Hay House, 2007.

Freund, Elizabeth. *The Return of the Reader: Reader-Response Criticism*. New York: Methuen, 1987.

Bibliography

Funk, Robert. *The Poetics of Biblical Narrative*. Sonoma: Polebridge, 1988.
Gathercole, Simon. *The Gospel of Judas: Rewriting Early Christian History*. Oxford: Oxford University Press, 2007.
Gaventa, Beverly Roberts. *Acts*. Nashville: Abingdon, 2003.
———. "Initiatives Divine and Human in the Lukan Story World." In *The Holy Spirit and Christian Origins*, edited by Graham N. Stanton, Bruce W. Longenecker, and Stephen C. Barton, 79–89. Grand Rapids: Eerdmans, 2004.
Gompertz, Rolf. *A Jewish Novel about Jesus*. New York: iUniverse, 2003.
Goodacre, Mark. *The Case against Q*. Harrisburg, PA: Trinity, 2002.
Graves, Robert. *King Jesus*. New York: Farrar, Strauss, and Giroux, 1946.
Green, Joel. "Good News to Whom? Jesus and the 'Poor' in the Gospel of Luke." In *Jesus of Nazareth: Lord and Christ*, edited by Joel B. Green and Max Turner, 59–74. Carlisle, UK: Paternoster, 1994.
———. *The Gospel of Luke*. Grand Rapids: Eerdmans, 1997.
Gregory, Andrew F. and C. Kavin Rowe, eds. *Rethinking the Unity and Reception of Luke and Acts*. Columbia: The University of South Carolina Press, 2010.
Gros Louis, Kenneth R. R. "The Jesus Birth Stories." In *Literary Interpretations of Biblical Narratives*, vol. 2, edited by Kenneth R. R. Gros Louis with James S. Ackerman, 273–84. Nashville: Abingdon, 1982.
Harrison, Marcus. *The Memoirs of Jesus Christ*. London: Arlington, 1975.
Harrison, Robert. *Oriel's Diary: An Archangel's Account of the Life of Jesus*. Bletchley, UK: Scripture Union, 2002.
Hays, Richard B. *The Moral Vision of the New Testament*. New York: HarperSanFrancisco, 1996.
Heym, Stefan. *Ahasver*. Gütersloh, Germany: Bertelsmann, 1981.
Holmes, Marjorie. *The Messiah*. San Francisco: Harper and Row, 1987.
Hornik, Heidi J., and Mikeal C. Parsons. *Illuminating Luke: The Infancy Narrative in Italian Renaissance*. Harrisburg, PA: Trinity, 2003.
———. *Illuminating Luke: The Public Ministry of Christ in Italian and Renaissance and Baroque Painting*. London: T. & T. Clark, 2005.
———. *Illuminating Luke: The Passion and Resurrection Narratives in Italian and Renaissance and Baroque Painting*. London: T. & T. Clark, 2008.
Horton, Dennis J. *Death and Resurrection: The Shape and Function of a Literary Motif in the Book of Acts*. Eugene, OR: Pickwick, 2009.
Hussein, M. Kamel. *City of Wrong: A Friday in Jerusalem*. 1957. Reprint. Oxford: Oneworld, 1994.
Iser, Wolfgang. *The Act of Reading: A Theory of Aesthetic Response*. Baltimore: Johns Hopkins University Press, 1978.
———. "The Reading Process: A Phenomenological Approach." *New Literary History* 3 (1972) 279–99.
Kassoff, David. *The Book of Witnesses*. London: Collins, 1971.
Kazantzakis, Nikos. *The Last Temptation*. London: Faber & Faber, 2003.
Kuecker, Aaron. *The Spirit and The "Other": Social Identity, Ethnicity, and Intergroup Reconciliation in Luke-Acts*. London: T. & T. Clark, 2011.

Bibliography

LaHaye, Tim, and Jerry B. Jenkins. *Mark's Story: The Gospel according to Peter.* New York: Berkley Praise, 2007.

Leaney, A. R. C. *A Commentary on the Gospel according to St. Luke.* London: Black, 1958.

Liddell, H. G., R. Scott, and H. S. Jones. *A Greek-English Lexicon*, 9th ed. with rev. suppl. Oxford: Clarendon, 1996.

Lincoln, Andrew. *Truth on Trial: The Lawsuit Motif in the Fourth Gospel.* Peabody, MA: Hendrickson, 2000.

Longenecker, Bruce W. "The Challenge of a Hopeless God: Negotiating José Saramago's Novel *The Gospel according to Jesus Christ*." In *Patterns of Promise: Art, Imagination, and Christian Hope*, edited by Trevor Hart, Gavin Hopps, and Jeremy Begbie, forthcoming. Aldershot, UK: Ashgate, 2012.

——— . *Rhetoric at the Boundaries: The Art and Theology of New Testament Chain-Link Transitions.* Waco, TX: Baylor University Press, 2005.

——— . "Rome's Victory and God's Honour: The Jerusalem Temple and the Spirit of God in Lukan Theodicy." In *The Holy Spirit and Christian Origins*, edited by Graham N. Stanton, Bruce W. Longenecker, and Stephen C. Barton, 90–102. Grand Rapids: Eerdmans, 2004.

Louw, J. P. and E. A. Nida. *Greek-English Lexicon of the New Testament, Based on Semantic Domains.* 2nd ed. New York: United Bible Society, 1988.

Mailer, Norman. *The Gospel according to the Son.* London: Abacus, 1997.

Mailloux, Steven. *Interpretive Conventions: The Reader in the Study of American Fiction.* Ithaca, NY: Cornell University Press, 1982.

Malbon, Elizabeth Struthers. "Echoes and Foreshadowings in Mark 4–8: Reading and Rereading." *Journal of Biblical Literature* 112 (1993) 213–32.

Marguerat, Daniel. *The First Christian Historian: Writing the "Acts of the Apostles".* Cambridge: Cambridge University Press, 2002.

Marshall, I. Howard. *The Gospel of Luke: A Commentary on the Greek Text.* Grand Rapids: Eerdmans, 1976.

Maxwell, Kathy Reiko. *Hearing between the Lines: The Audience as Fellow-Worker in Luke-Acts and its Literary Milieu.* London: T. & T. Clark, 2010.

Merchant, Moelwyn. *Jeshua.* Allison Park, PA: Pickwick, 1987.

Meynet, Roland. *L'Évangile de Luc.* Paris: Lethielleux, 2005.

——— . *L'Évangile selon saint Luc.* Paris: Cerf, 1988.

Moberly, Walter. *From Eden to Golgotha: Essays in Biblical Theology.* Atlanta: Scholars, 1992.

Moessner, David P. "'Managing the Audience': The Rhetoric of Authorial Intent and Audience Comprehension in the Narrative Epistemology of Polybius of Megalopolis, Diodorus Siculus, and Luke the Evangelist." In *The Word Leaps the Gap: Essays on Scripture and Theology in Honor of Richard B. Hays*, edited by J. Ross Wagner, C. Kavin Rowe, and A. Katherine Grieb, 179–97. Grand Rapids: Eerdmans, 2008.

Bibliography

———. "Reading Luke's Gospel as Ancient Hellenistic Narrative." In *Reading Luke: Interpretation, Reflection, Formation*, edited by C. Bartholomew, J. B. Green, and A. C. Thiselton, 125-54. Carlisle, UK: Paternoster, 2005.

Monhollon, Michael. *Divine Invasion*. Abilene, TX: Reflection, 1998.

Mossinsohn, Igal. *Judas*. New York: St. Martin's, 1963.

O'Brien, Michael D. *Theophilus: A Novel*. San Francisco: Ignatius, 2010.

Omanson, Roger L. *A Textual Guide to the Greek New Testament*. Stuttgart: German Bible Society, 2006.

Parsons, Mikeal C. *Acts*. Grand Rapids: Baker Academic, 2008.

Perrin, Nicholas. *Thomas: The Other Gospel*. London: SPCK, 2007.

Plummer, Alfred. *A Critical and Exegetical Commentary on the Gospel according to S. Luke*. Edinburgh: T. & T. Clark, 1896.

Pollock, John. *The Apostle*. London: Hodder & Stoughton, 1969.

Puskas, Charles B. *The Conclusion of Luke-Acts: The Significance of Acts 28:16-31*. Eugene, OR: Pickwick, 2009.

Ricci, Nino. *Testament*. New York: Houghton Mifflin, 2003.

Rice, Anne. *The Road to Cana*. London: Chatto & Windus, 2008.

Ricoeur, Paul. *Interpretation Theory: Discourse and the Surplus of Meaning*. Fort Worth, TX: Texas Christian University Press, 1976.

Rowe, C. Kavin. *Early Narrative Christology: The Lord in the Gospel of Luke*. Grand Rapids: Baker Academic, 2009.

Saramago, José. *The Gospel according to Jesus Christ*. San Diego: Harcourt Brace, 1993.

Sayers, Dorothy L. *The Man Born to be King*. 1943. Reprint. San Francisco: Ignatius, 1990.

Schnelle, Udo. *Theology of the New Testament*. Translated by M. Eugene Boring. Grand Rapids: Baker Academic, 2009.

Schürmann, Heinz. *Das Lukasevangelium*, vol. 1. Freiburg: Herder, 1969.

Smith, Christian. "Five Proposals for Reforming Article Publishing in the Social Scientific Study of Religion (Especially Quantitative): Improving the Quality, Value, and Cumulativeness of our Scholarship." *Journal for the Scientific Study of Religion* 49 (2010) 583-95.

Squires, John T. *The Plan of God in Luke-Acts*. Cambridge: Cambridge University Press, 1993.

Sternberg, Meir. *The Poetics of Biblical Narrative: Ideological Literature and the Drama of Reading*. Bloomington, IN: Indiana University Press, 1985.

Strelan, Rick. *Strange Acts: Studies in the Cultural World of the Acts of the Apostles*. New York: de Gruyter, 2004.

Talbert, Charles H. *Reading Luke*. London: SPCK, 1982.

Thayer, J. H. *A Greek-English Lexicon of the New Testament*. Reprint. Peabody, MA: Hendrickson, 1996.

Thoene, Brodie, and Brock Thoene. *The Jerusalem Scrolls*. New York: Penguin, 2002.

Tiede, D. L. "Glory to Thy People Israel." In *Luke-Acts and the Jewish People*, edited by J. B. Tyson, 21-34. Minneapolis: Augsburg, 1988.

Bibliography

Tolkien, J. R. R. *The Letters of J. R. R. Tolkien*. Edited by Humphrey Carpenter. Boston: Houghton Mifflin, 1981.

———. "On Fairy-Stories." In his *Tree and Leaf,* 11–72. Reprint. London: Grafton, 1992.

Tompkins, Jane P., ed. *Reader-Response Criticism: From Formalism to Post-Structuralism*. Baltimore: Johns Hopkins University Press, 1980.

Wangerin, Walter. *The Book of God: The Bible as a Novel*. Grand Rapids: Zondervan, 1996.

———. *Jesus: A Novel*. Oxford: Lion, 2005.

———. *Paul: A Novel*. Oxford: Lion, 2000.

Watson, Francis. *A Guide to the New Testament*. London: Batsford, 1987.

Whitlark, Jason A., and Mikeal C. Parsons. "The 'Seven' Last Words: A Numerical Motivation for the Insertion of Luke 23.34a." *New Testament Studies* 52 (2006) 188–204.

Wright, N. T. *Judas and the Gospel of Jesus: Have We Missed the Truth about Christianity?* Grand Rapids: Baker, 2006.

Index of Ancient Sources

OLD TESTAMENT

Genesis
1	75
3:15	87n5, 93n13
22	81n15

Exodus
14	75

Deuteronomy
6:16	86

1 Kings
5:14	85n1
17:1	85n1
17:8–9	85n1
17:17–24	54
18:1–2	85n1

2 Kings
5:1–14	54

Psalms
2:7	100
22:18	101
31:5	101
80	80–81
90:13	121
91	84, 86–87, 87n5, 88, 88n6, 91n11, 91n12, 93, 98, 105, 107, 109, 121
91:11	87, 89–90, 96
91:11–12	85, 86, 86n3, 86n3, 87–89, 92, 94, 94n13, 95–96, 98, 99n23, 101, 109–10, 117–18, 120–23
91:13	86n3, 87, 87n5, 93n13, 95n16, 120–23
110:1	101
118:22	100
118:26	100

Isaiah
61	15, 53

NEW TESTAMENT

Matthew
	87, 88n6
1:18—2:23	2
4:5–7	85
4:6	87
4:11	87
12:46–50	32
13:53–58	21
15:4	101n25
15:8–10	101

Matthew (cont.)

15:11–32	101
18:12–14	101
20:20–21	5n5
23:29	100
26:39	90n10

Mark

	15, 21, 87, 88n6, 100
1:11	100
1:12–13	87
1:13	87
1:17	4
1:18	4
1:20	4
1:29–31	4
3:31–35	32
6:1–6	34n14
6:3	34n14
6:3–6	14
6:4	34n14
10:25–27	5n5
12:10–11	100
12:28–31	103
12:46	101
15:24	101

Luke

	31, 87, 88, 93, 100
1	62–63
1:1	99
1:5	6
1:5–56	61
1:6	51n24
1:18	62
1:20	62n1
1:26–56	2
1:34	62n1
1:37	62
1:39	51n24
1:79	64

2:1–40	2
2:3	51n24
2:30	68
2:41	51n24
2:41–52	2
3:1–2	64
3:6	68
3:18–20	6
3:19–20	64
3:22	100
4	24, 32, 43, 54, 62–63, 76, 85, 118
4:1–4	97n20
4:1–13	84, 98
4:4	84
4:5–8	97n20
4:8	84
4:9–11	85
4:9–12	85
4:10	89, 96
4:10–11	88–89, 96, 97n18, 98–99, 105, 107, 109, 110
4:12	84, 86
4:13	87, 94, 97
4:14–44	52
4:14–15	48n19, 52, 84, 98n22
4:16–20	84
4:16–30	14, 52, 55, 95, 98, 98n22
4:17	85
4:18	97n18
4:21	34n14
4:22	34n14
4:23	19n7
4:24	34n14
4:25–27	85n1
4:28	41
4:28–29	15–17, 23, 26, 52

Index of Ancient Sources

Luke (cont.)

4:28–30	9, 14, 23–25, 35, 49–50, 56, 58, 61, 113, 116
4:29	17, 17n4
4:30	xiv, 9, 14–15, 17–19, 21, 23, 25, 30, 37–38, 42–43, 43n9, 44–47, 49–51, 56, 58–59, 60, 62–64, 66, 70, 71, 72, 83, 84, 95, 96, 97n18, 99, 101, 105, 107–10, 116–18
4:31	99n23
4:31–41/42	52
4:38–40	4
4:38—5:11	4
4:40–41	5
4:42	52
4:43	52
4:44	52
5:1–11	5, 18, 102
5:8	102
5:10	4–5
5:12–16	102
7:1–10	54
7:11–15	54
7:15	54n26
8:19–21	32
9:1	121
9:7–9	6
9:12–17	97n20
9:36	51
9:51	51, 120
9:51–53	50
9:51–56	120
9:51—10:42	120, 122
9:51—13:21	120
9:51—19:10	51
9:57	50–51
9:57—10:11	120
10:12–16	120
10:17–20	120–22
10:19	95n16, 121–23
10:21–24	120
10:25–37	120
10:25–42	102
10:27	103
10:29	103
10:30–37	103
10:38	50–51
10:38–42	103, 120
13:31–33	50
13:31	6
13:32	6
13:33	51, 122
13:35	100
15	101
15:1–7	101
15:6	101n25
15:8–9	101n25
15:17	101n25
15:24	101n25
15:32	101n25
16	100
16:16	100
16:29	100
16:31	100
17:11	50–51
18:31	51
19:28	50–51
20:17	100
20:20–26	4n3
20:42–43	101
21:38	120
22:3	4n3, 93n13
22:22	51
22:31	4n3
22:39	90
22:43	91n11
22:43–44	90–94, 97n19, 118

Luke (cont.)

22:44	91, 91n11, 94
23–24	55
23:12	6
23:3	6
23:6–16	6
23:34	49, 101
23:35	83
23:37	83
23:37–38	6
23:39–43	3
23:46	101
23:48	5
24:26	97n20
24:27	100
24:44	99
24:51	89n8

John

8	79
8:2–11	78
8:59	63n2
10:39	63n2
18:6	82

Acts

	19, 45, 46, 99
1:3	68
1:9	89, 89n8
1:9–11	89
1:10–11	89
1:11	89n8
1:16–20	99n24
2:16–21	99n24
2:36	41
5:17–24	56
5:19	57
5:21–24	57
7	17n4
7:54–60	65n5
7:58	17n4
8:26	59
8:26–40	59
8:39–40	59
9:36–42	58
12:6–11	56
13–19	48n20
13–28	67
14	58, 17n4
14:19–20	58, 59n35, 60, 113–14, 116
14:20–21	114
16:25–26	57, 60
20:7–12	58
25:11	67
27–28	115
28	67, 69, 122
28:1–6	59–60, 121
28:5	122
28:17	69
28:19	67
28:23	68
28:25–28	99n24
28:26–27	69
28:28	68
28:30–31	67
28:31	68

Revelation

1:3	106

~

EARLY CHRISTIAN LITERATURE

Augustine

On the Psalms

91	86n3, 89

Gospel of Judas	8
Gospel of Thomas	8

Index of Ancient Sources

Infancy Gospel of Thomas
2.1–5   2n1
3.1—4.1   2n1

Irenaeus
Against Heresies
3.23.7   86n3

John Chrysostom
Homilies on the Acts of the Apostles
15   70

Pseudo-Ignatius
Letter to the Philippians
§10   86n3

Syriac Diatessaron
113   99n23

Tertulian
Against Marcion
4   86n3

Against Praxeas
1   86n3

OTHER ANCIENT LITERATURE

Life of Issa
8.23–24   50n22

Index of Authors

Alter, R., 11
Appleby, J. O., 12
Archer, J., 34–35
Asch, S., 7

Baarda, T., 99
Barclay, W., 74–76
Barthes, R., 11
Bauckham, R., 88, 106–7
Beavis, M. A., 47
The Bible and Culture
    Collective, 10, 41
Boring, M. E., 87
Boyd, N., 27–28, 37
Brown, R. E., 91
Bultmann, R., 10

Campbell, D. A., 47
Cannon, J., 114
Chapman, S. B., 115
Chilton, B., 30–31, 33, 37,
    114–15
Clivaz, C., 91, 94
Coleridge, M., 18–19
Culy, M. C., 43
Cunningham, S., 17, 45–46

Donahue, J. R., 103–4
Dunn, J. D. G., 115

Ehrman, B. D., 90

Esler, P. F., 12–13
Evans, C. A., 54

Fish, S. E., 39
Fisk, B. N., 51
Fitzmyer, J. A., 51
Flynn, E. A., 39
Fortney, S., 8
Freke, T., 8
Freund, E., 39
Funk, R., 39

Gandy, P., 8
Gathercole, S., 8
Gaventa, B. R., 43, 115
Gompertz, R., 7, 21, 35
Goodacre, M., 3, 88
Graves, R., 8, 28–30, 37, 81
Green, J., 53, 95, 108
Gregory, A. F., 45
Gros Louis, K. R. R., 19

Harrison, M., 8, 34–37
Harrison, R., 16, 72–74
Hays, R. B., 11
Heym, S., 7
Holmes, M., 31–33, 37, 49
Hornik, H. J., 24
Horton, D. J., 59
Hussein, M. K., 7

Index of Authors

Iser, W., 20, 40–41, 107

Jenkins, J. B., 4

Kassoff, D., 7, 28, 35, 37
Kazantzakis, N., 22, 31–33, 37
Kuecker, A., 98, 118

LaHaye, T., 4
Leaney, A. R. C., 95, 108
Liddell, H. G., 94
Lincoln, A., 69
Longenecker, B. W., ix–x, 8, 44–45, 48, 108
Louw, J. P., 89

Mailer, N., 21, 35–36
Mailloux, S., 39
Malbon, E. S., 47
Marguerat, D., 20, 68–70
Marshall, I. H., 46
Maxwell, K. R., 19–21
Merchant, M., 75–76
Meynet, R., 93, 120–22
Moberly, W., 94
Moessner, D. P., 13, 46, 55
Monhollon, M., 16, 74, 109–10
Mossinsohn, I., 7
Murdoch, I., ix

Nida, E. A., 89

O' Brien, M. D., 27
Omanson, R. L., 49, 90

Parsons, M. C., 24, 49, 58
Perrin, N., 8
Plummer, A., 43
Pollock, J., 113–14
Puskas, C. B., 70

Ricci, N., 8
Rice, A., 16
Ricoeur, P., 11
Rowe, C. K., xi, 40, 45, 102

Saramago, J., 8
Sayers, D. L., 7
Schnelle, U., 45
Schürmann, H., 46, 95, 108
Schweickart, P. P., 39
Shakespeare, W., 85
Smith, C., 38
Squires, J. T., 45, 54
Sternberg, M., 20, 39, 43–44
Strelan, R., 56–60

Talbert, C. H., 45, 56
Thayer, J. H., 94
Thoene, B. & B., 76–83
Tiede, D. L., 68
Tolkien, J. R. R., 64–66
Tompkins, J. P., 39

Wangerin, W., 25–28, 37, 58, 93–94, 116
Watson, F., 13, 87
Whitlark, J. A., 49
Wright, N. T., 8

www.ingramcontent.com/pod-product-compliance
Lightning Source LLC
Chambersburg PA
CBHW020853160426
43192CB00007B/909